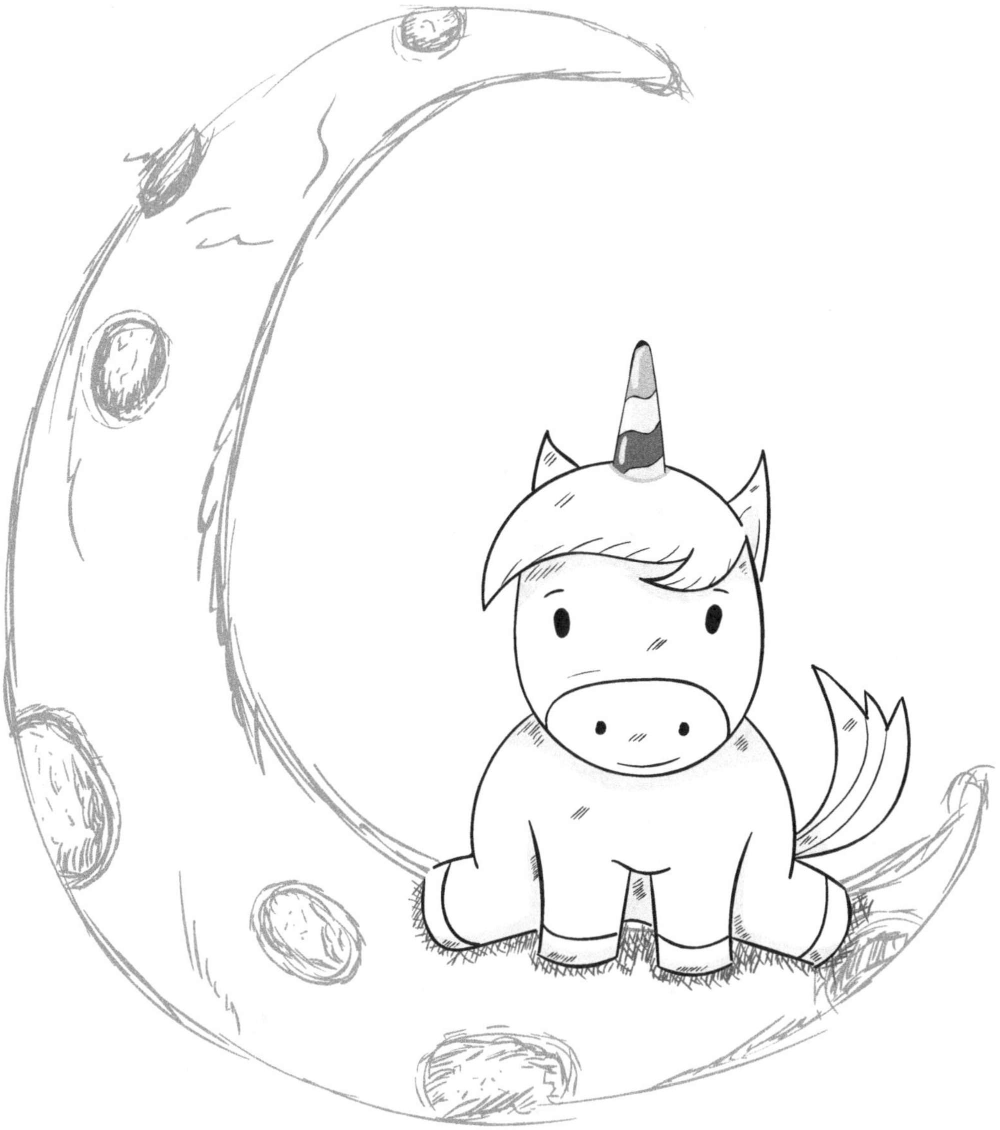

UNICORN COLORING BOOK

FOR KIDS

BY

Lucy Charm

PUBLISHED BY LUCY CHARM

PUBLISHED IN USA

ISBN-13: 978-1717405814

ISBN-10: 1717405819

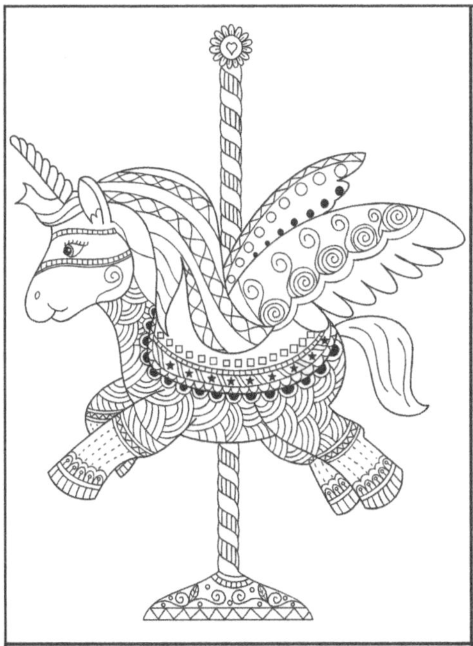

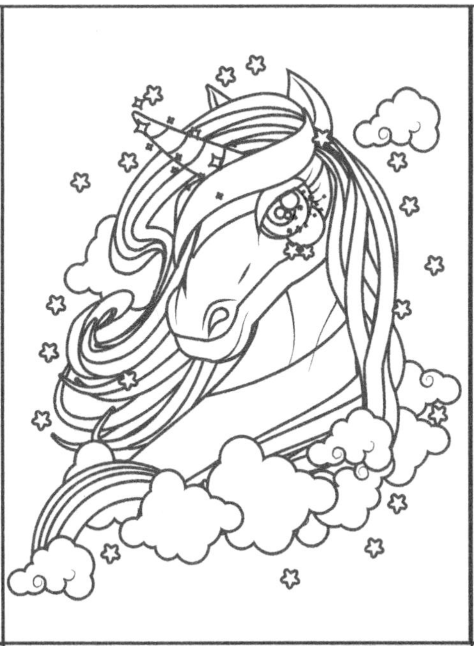

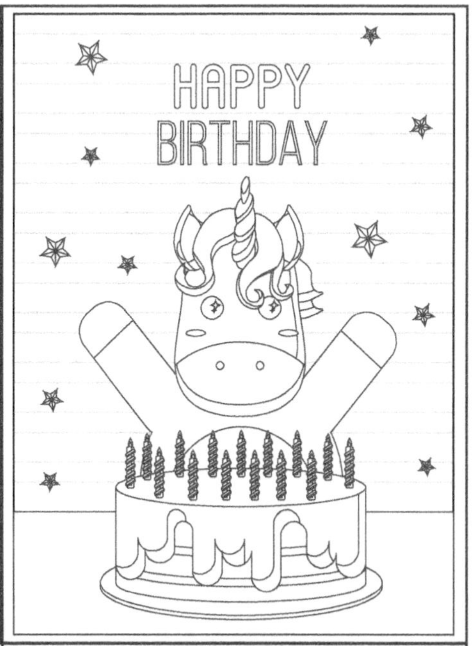
HAPPY
BIRTHDAY

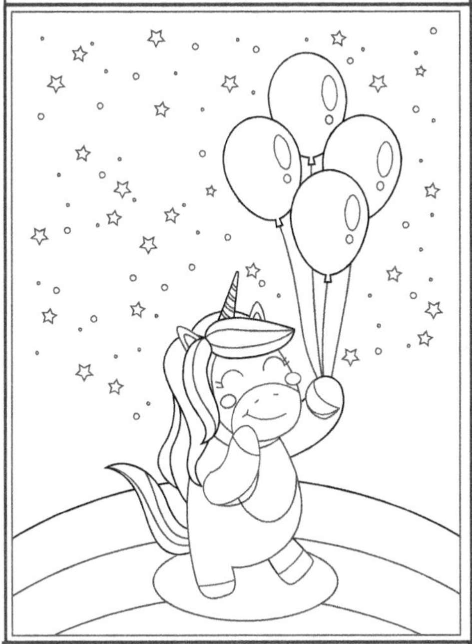

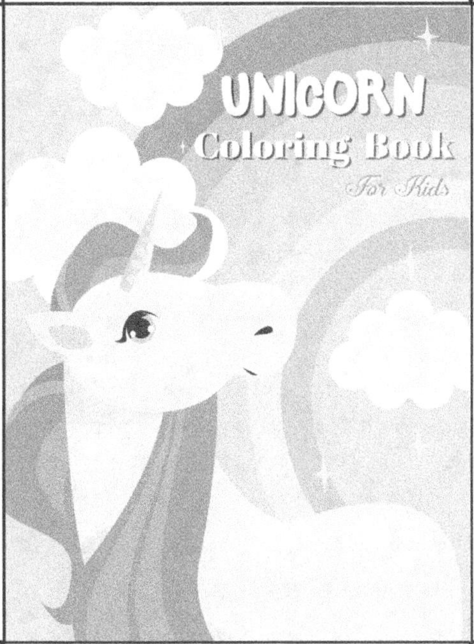
UNICORN
Coloring Book
For Kids

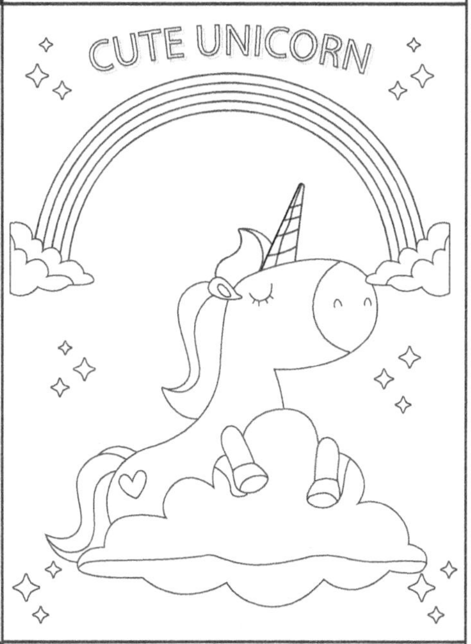
CUTE UNICORN

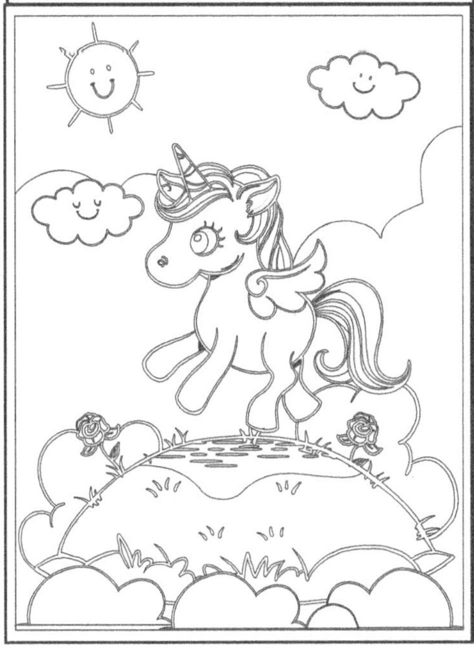

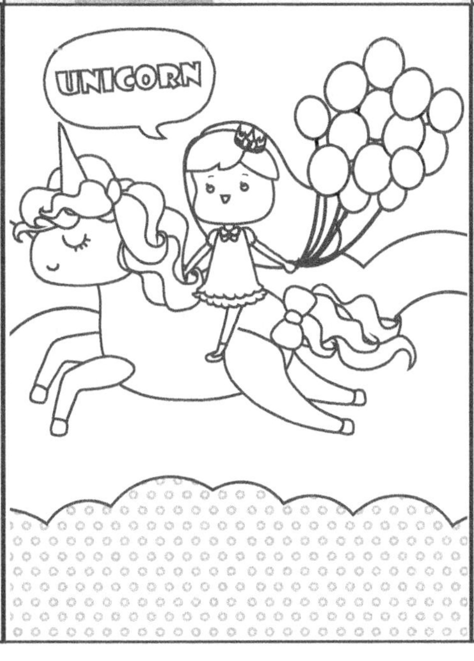
UNICORN

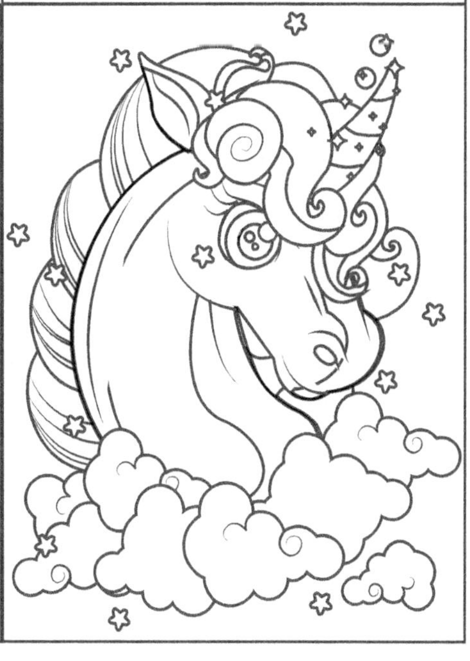

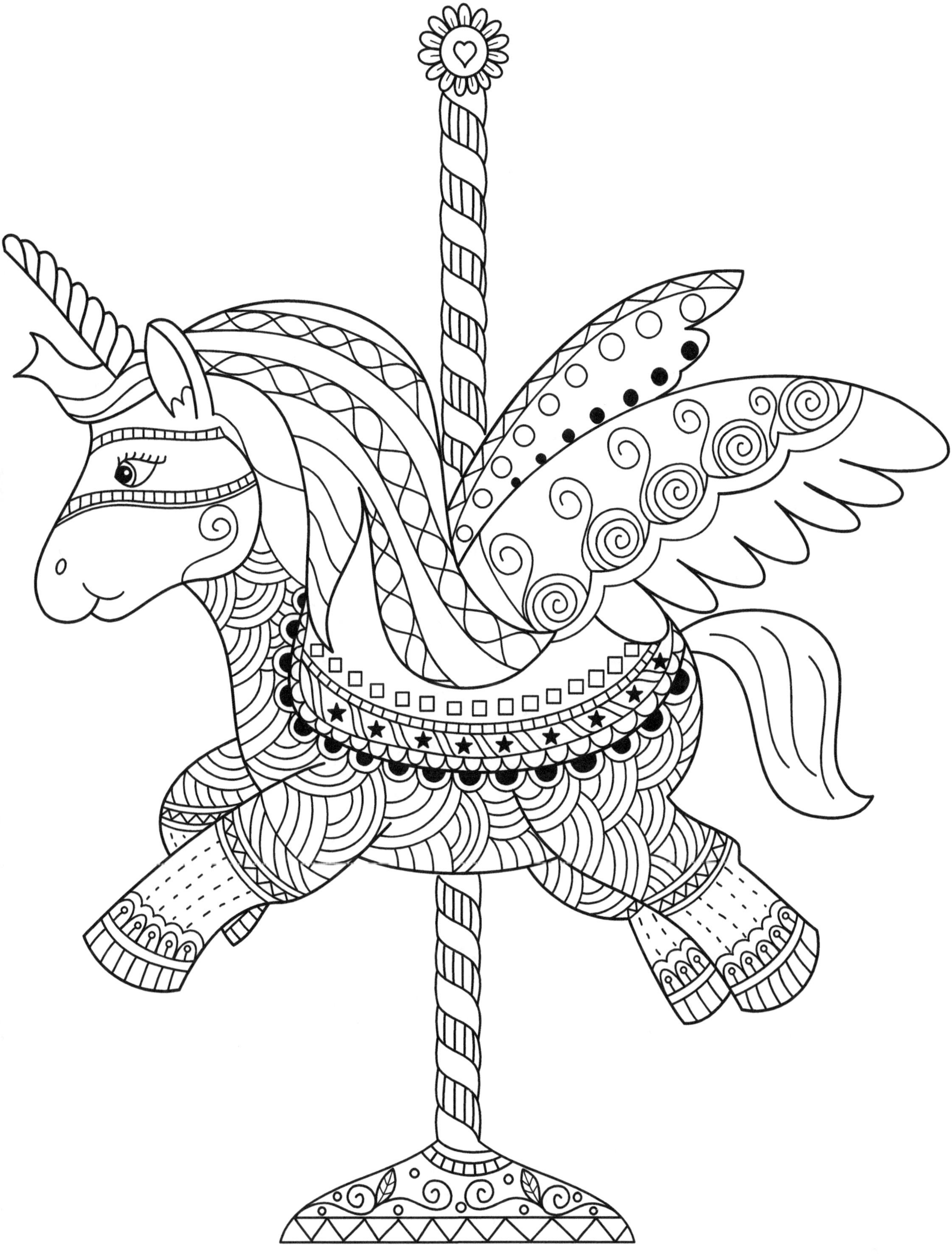

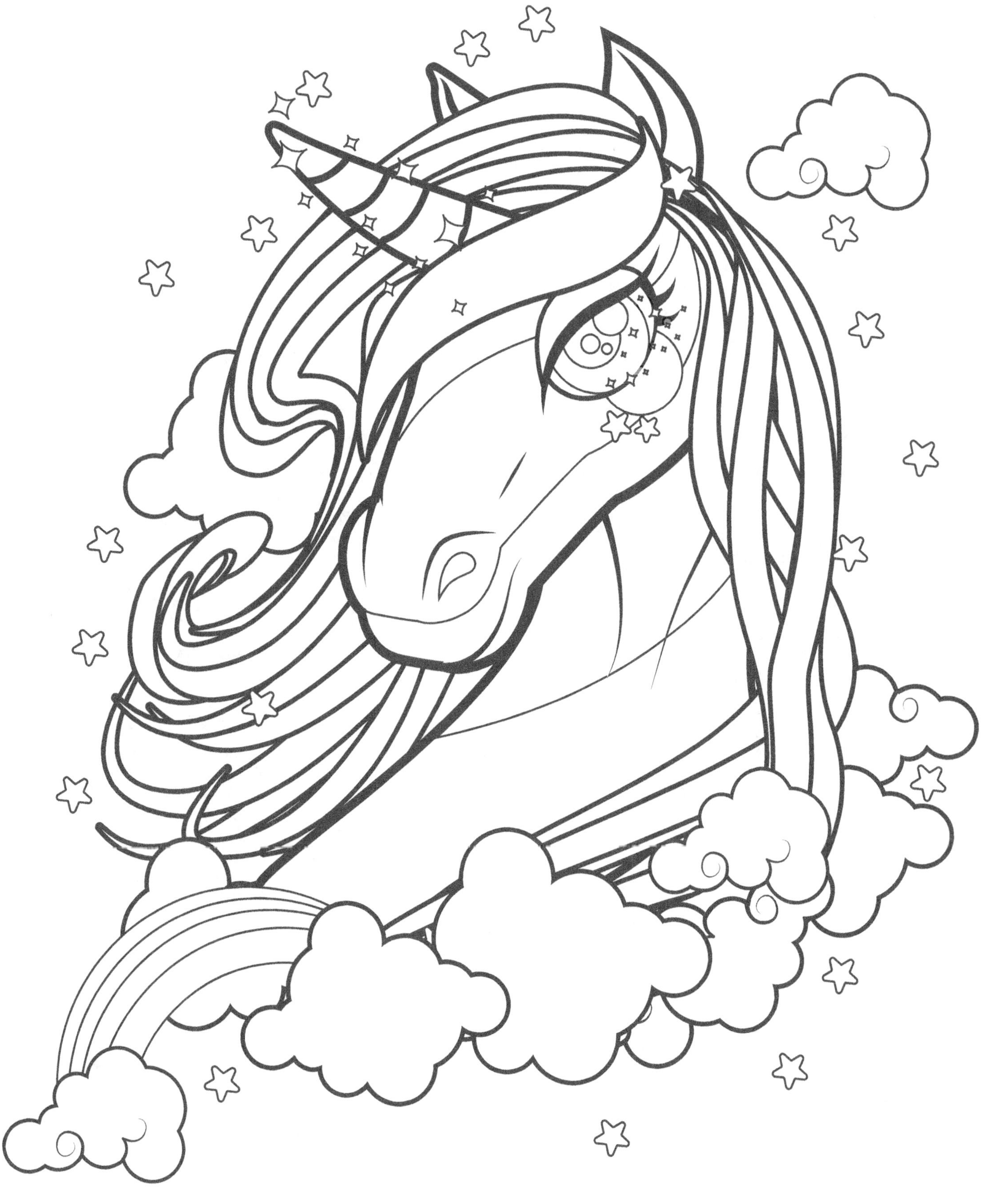

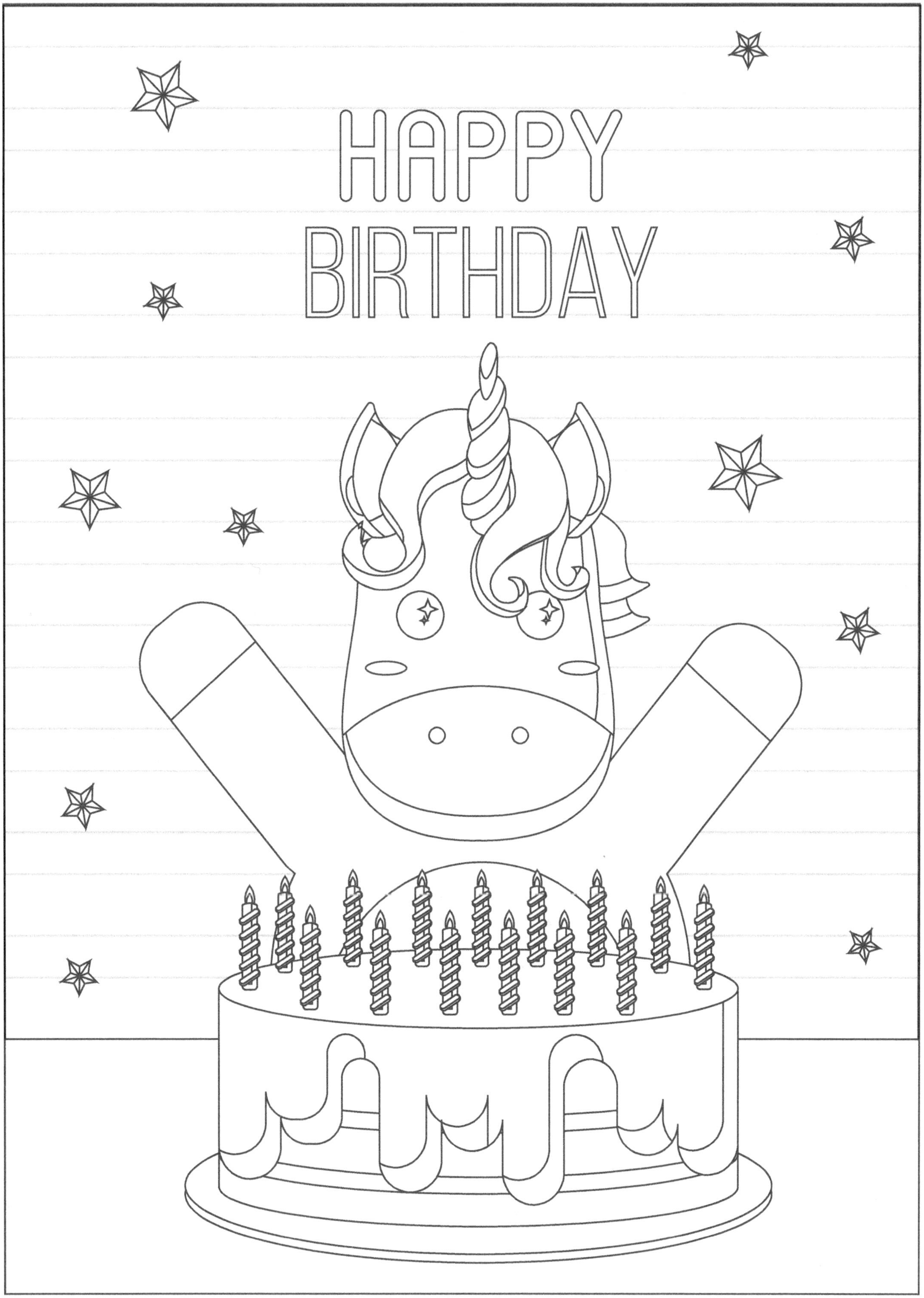
HAPPY
BIRTHDAY

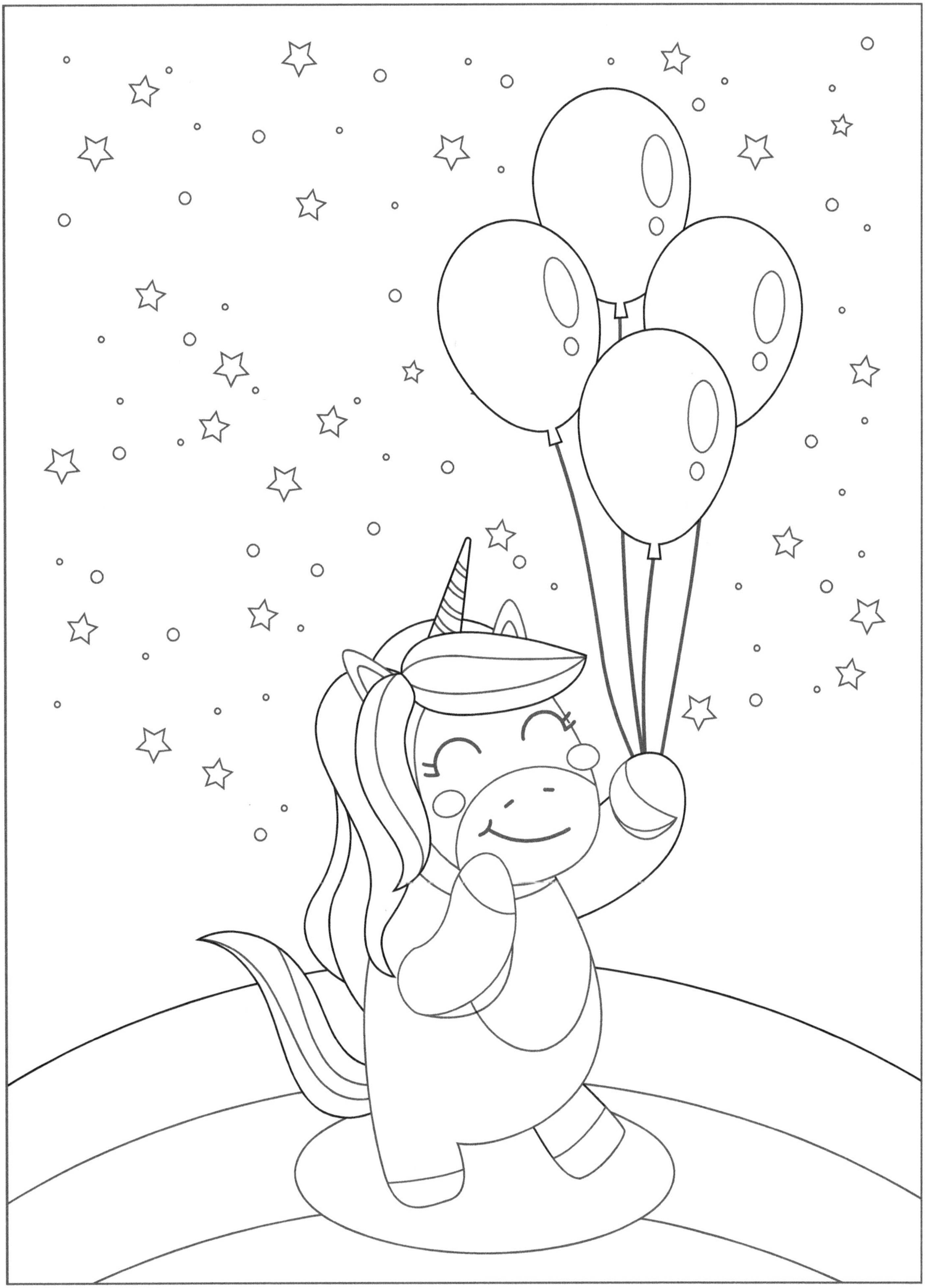

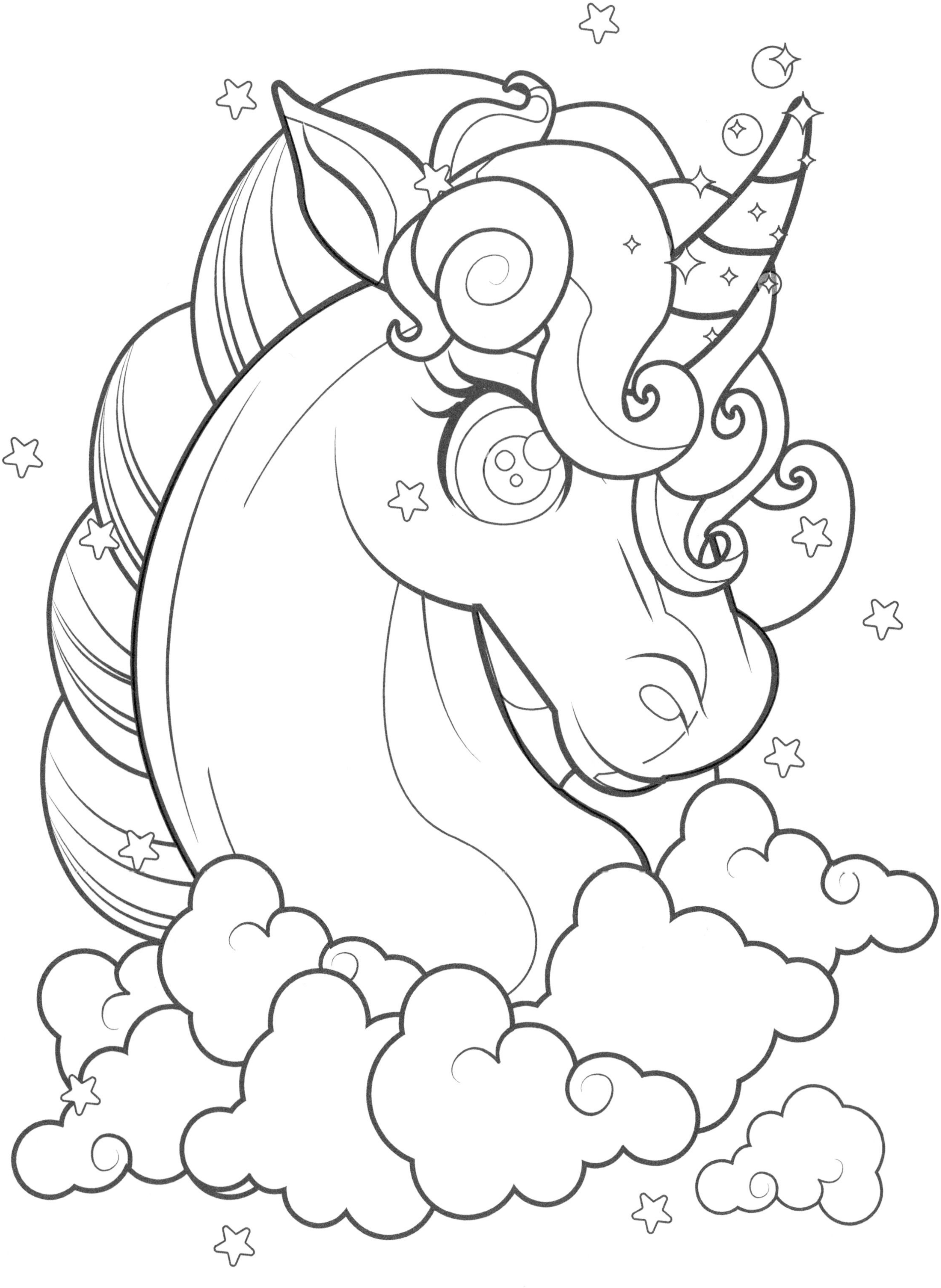

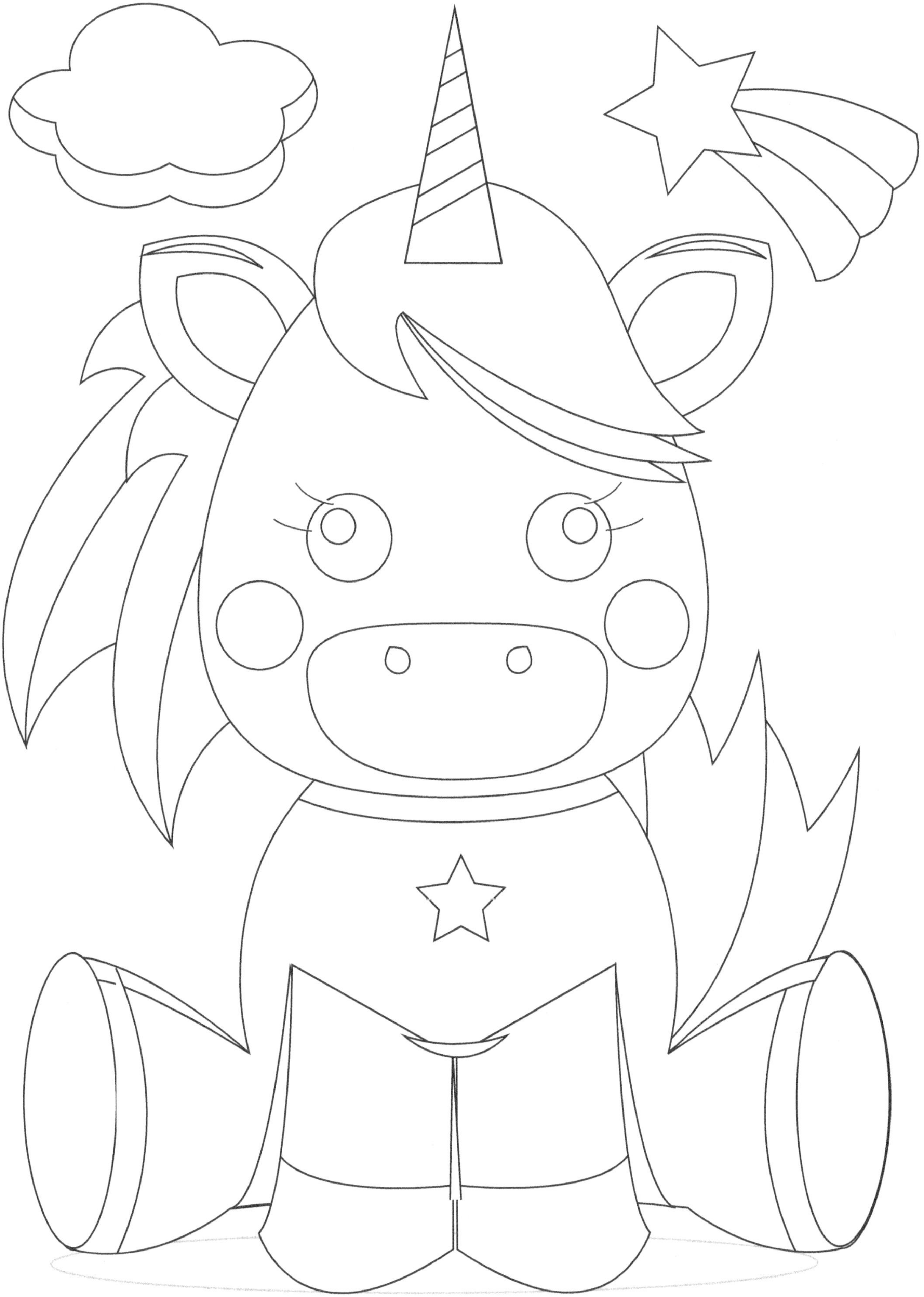

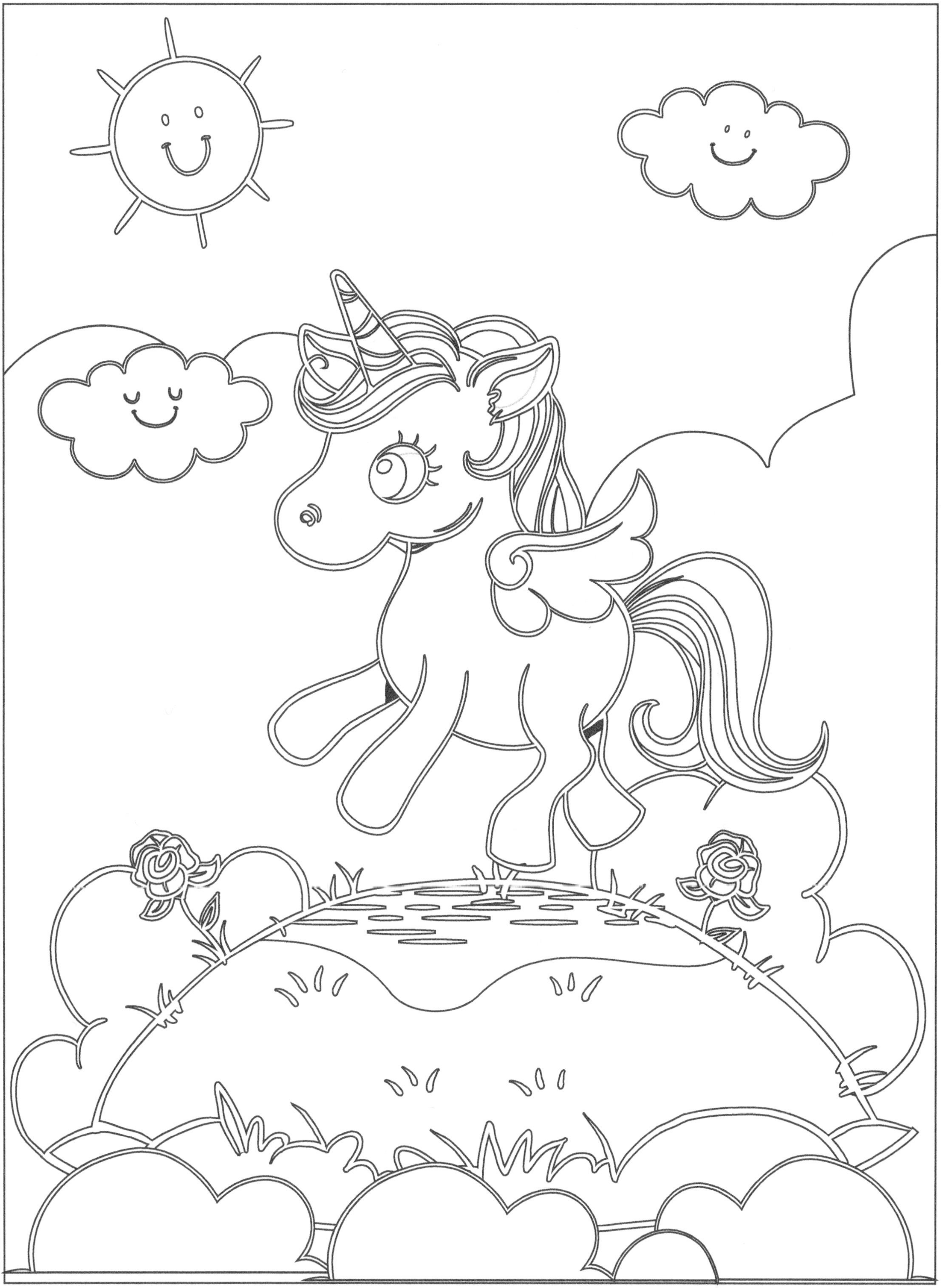

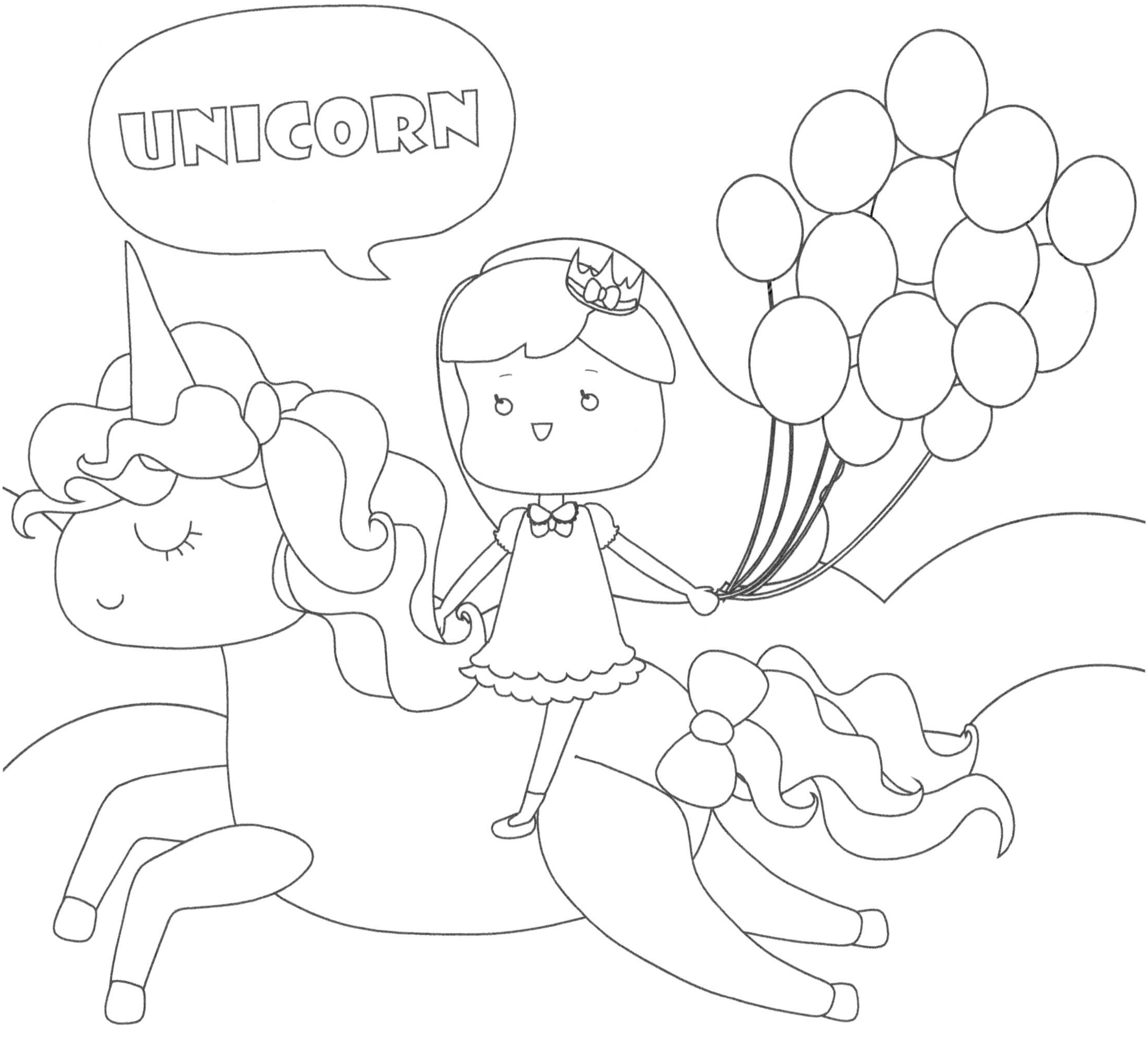
UNICORN

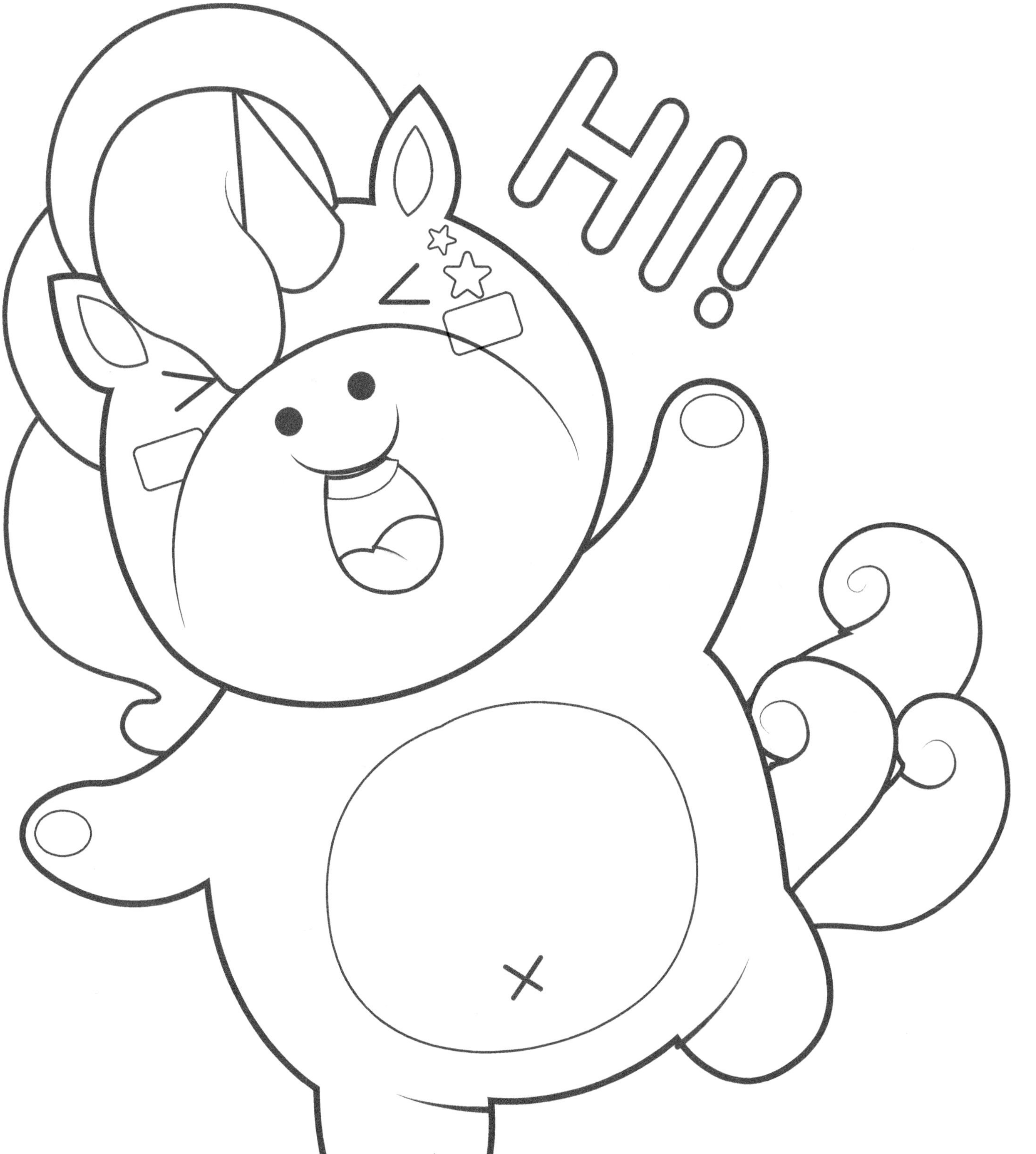
HI!!

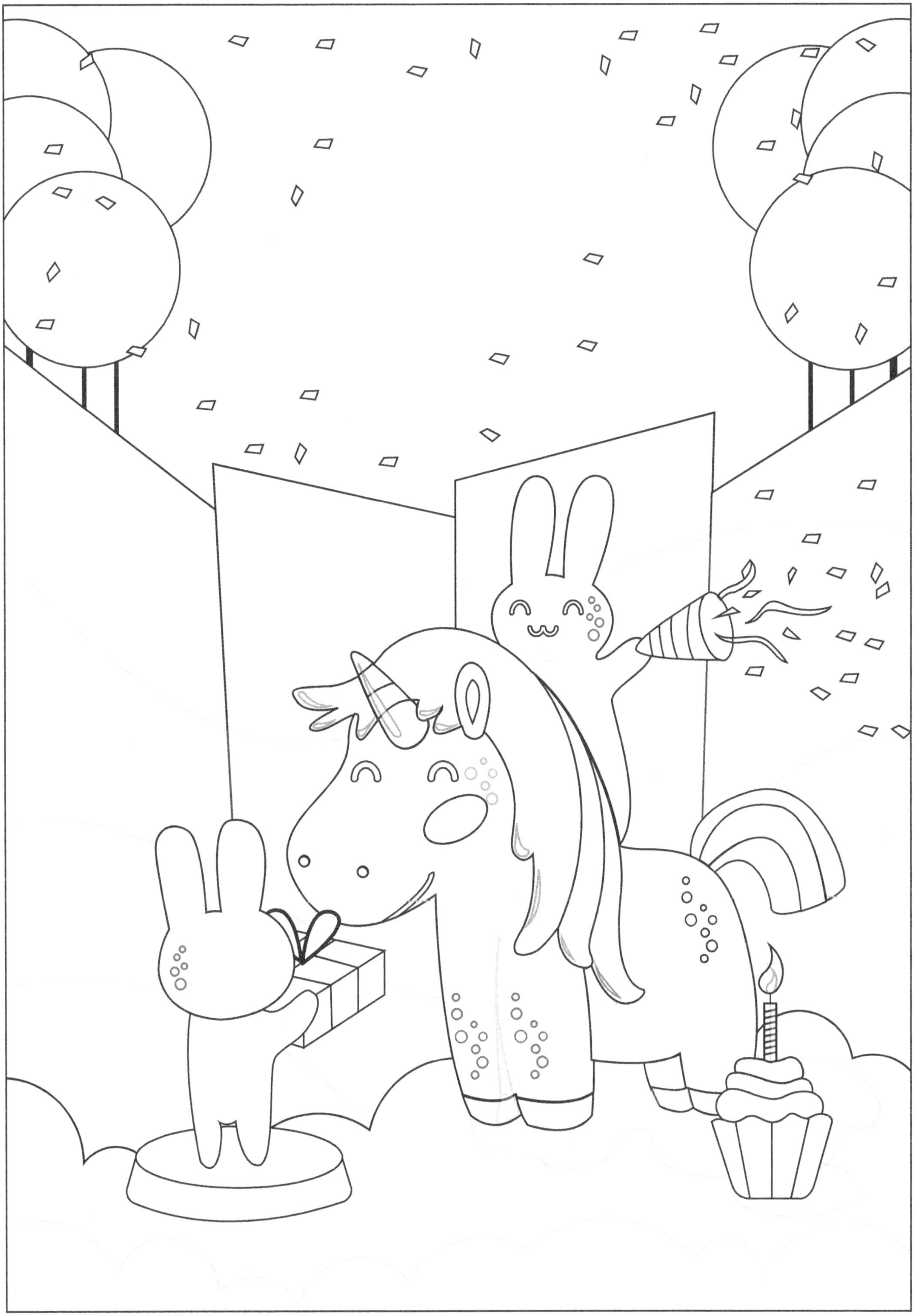

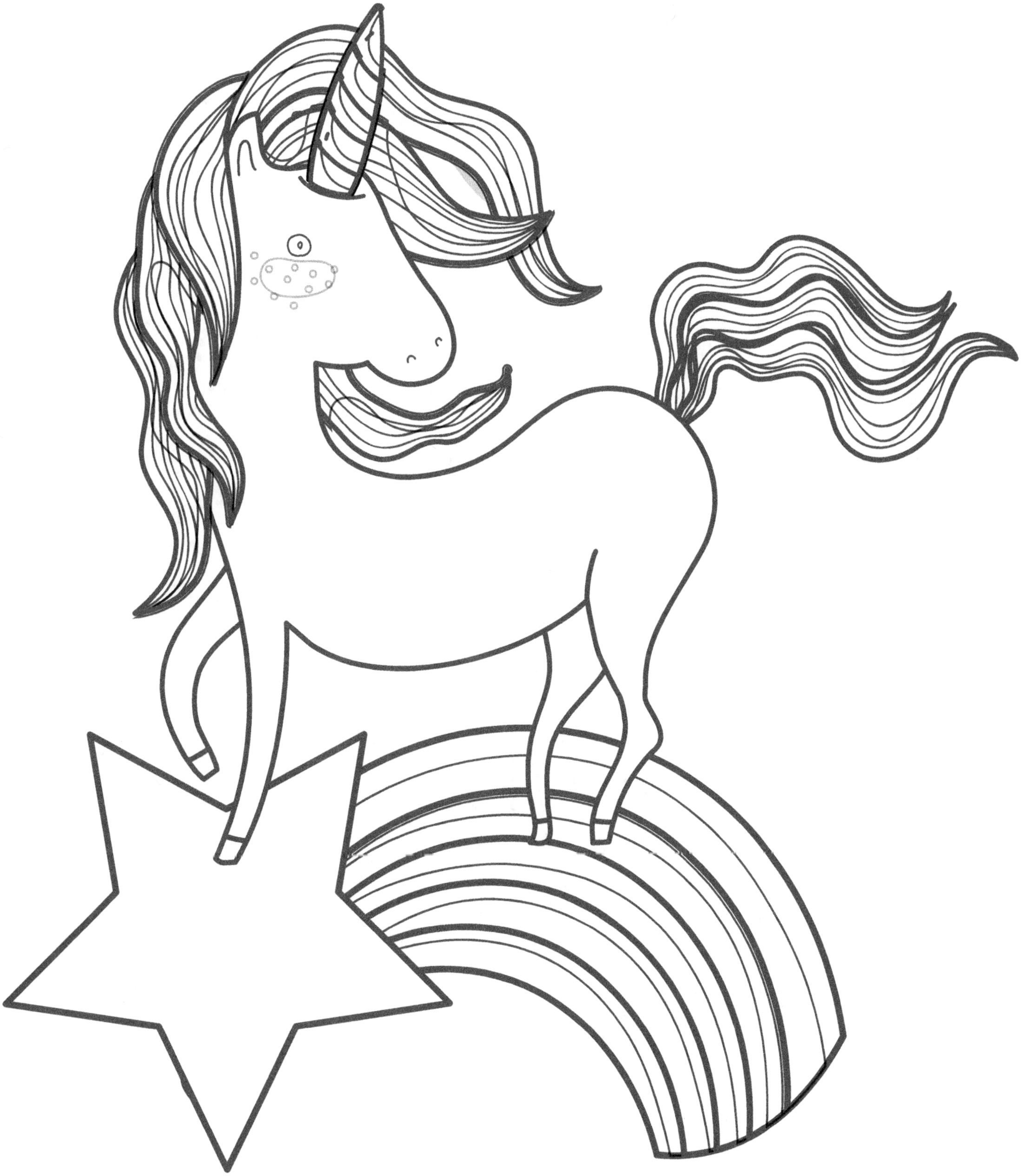

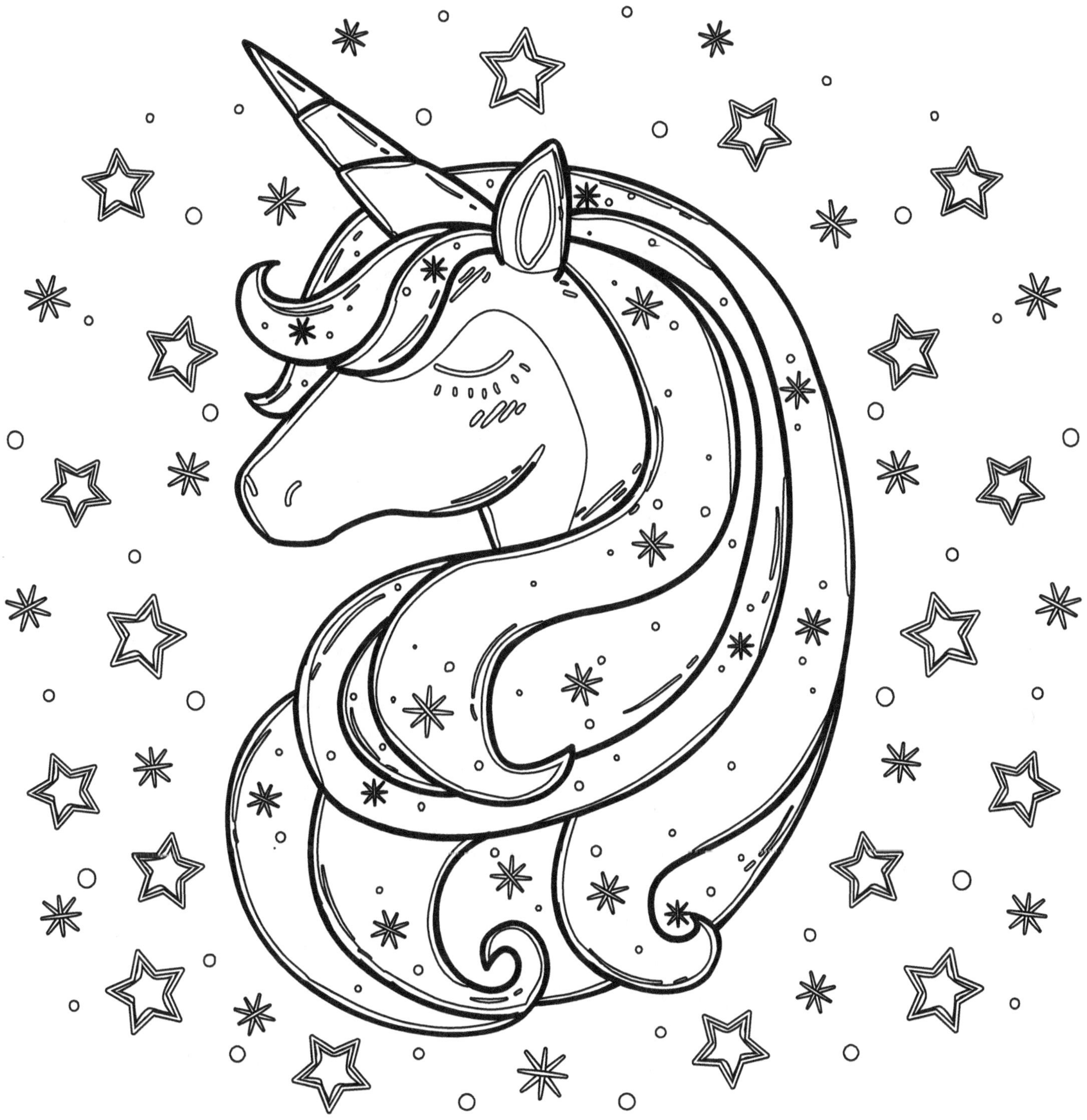

CUTE UNICORN

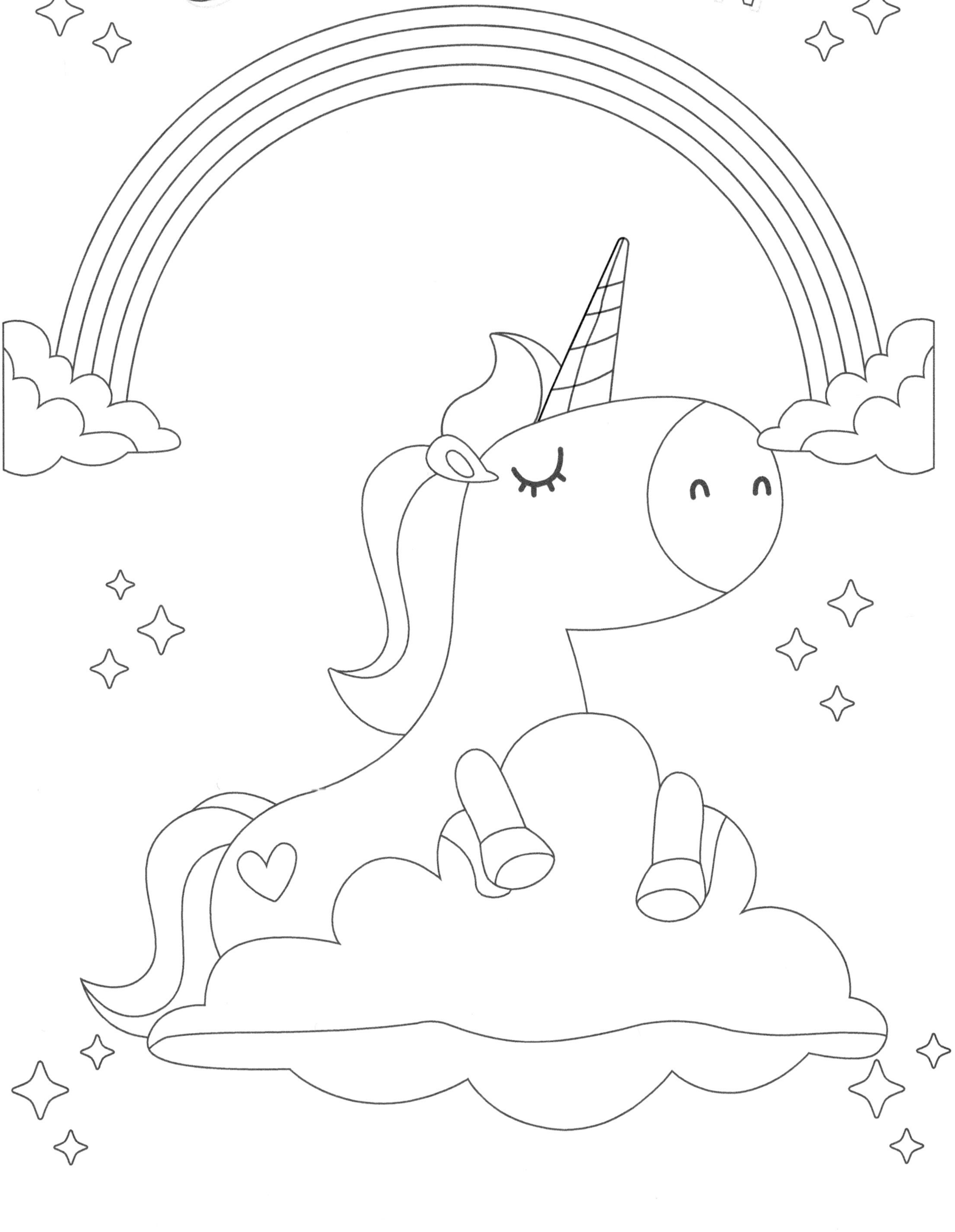

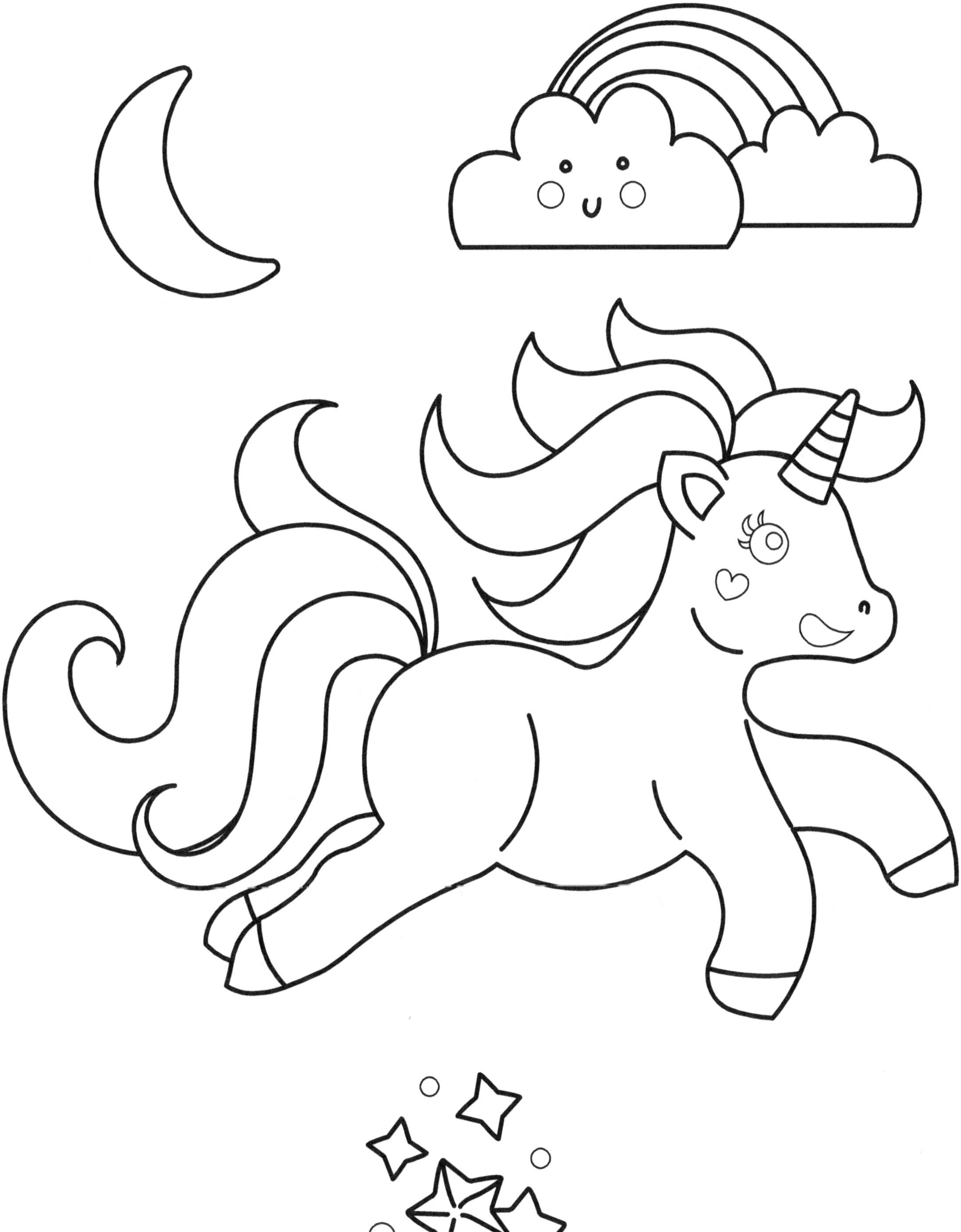

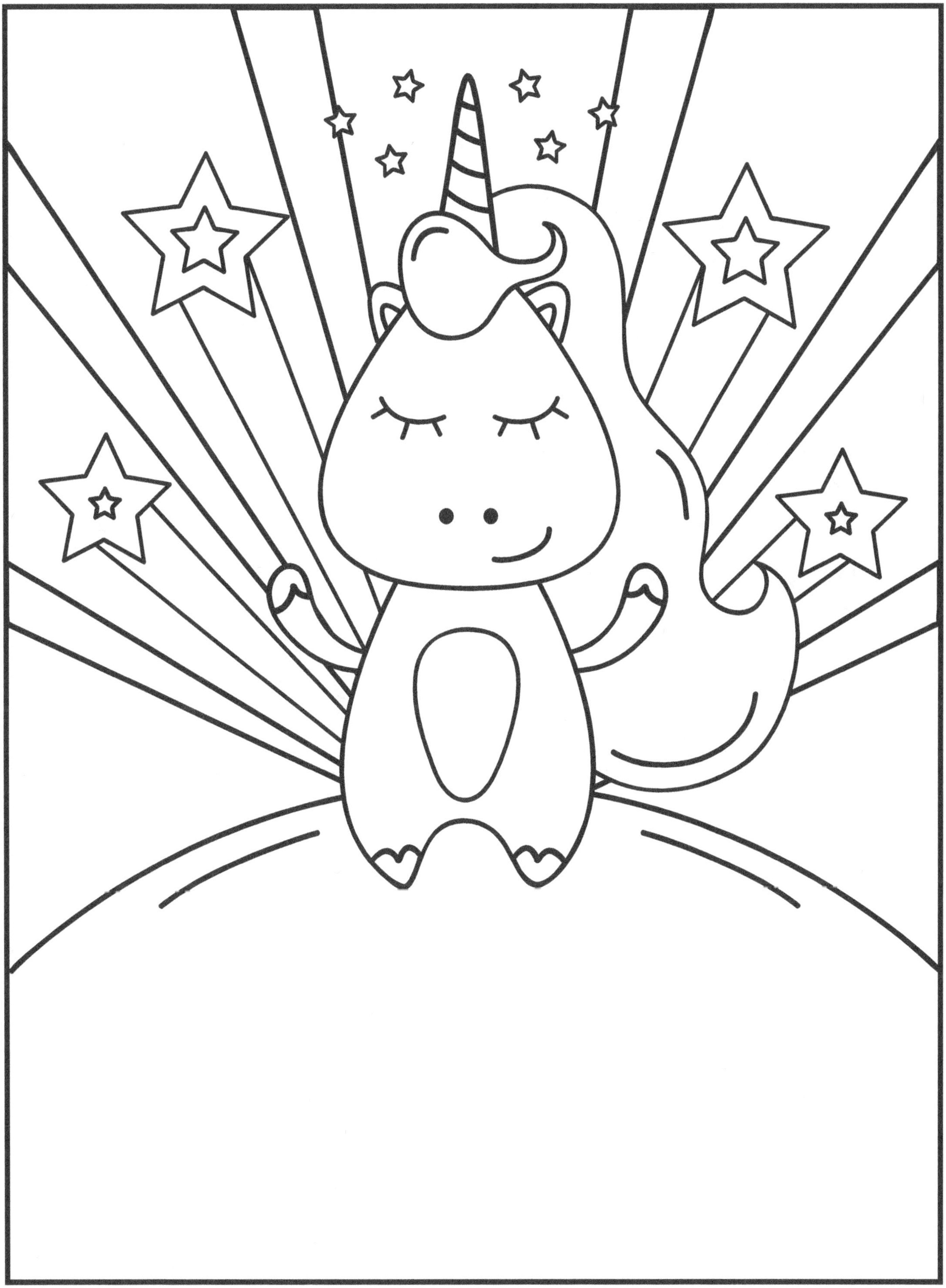

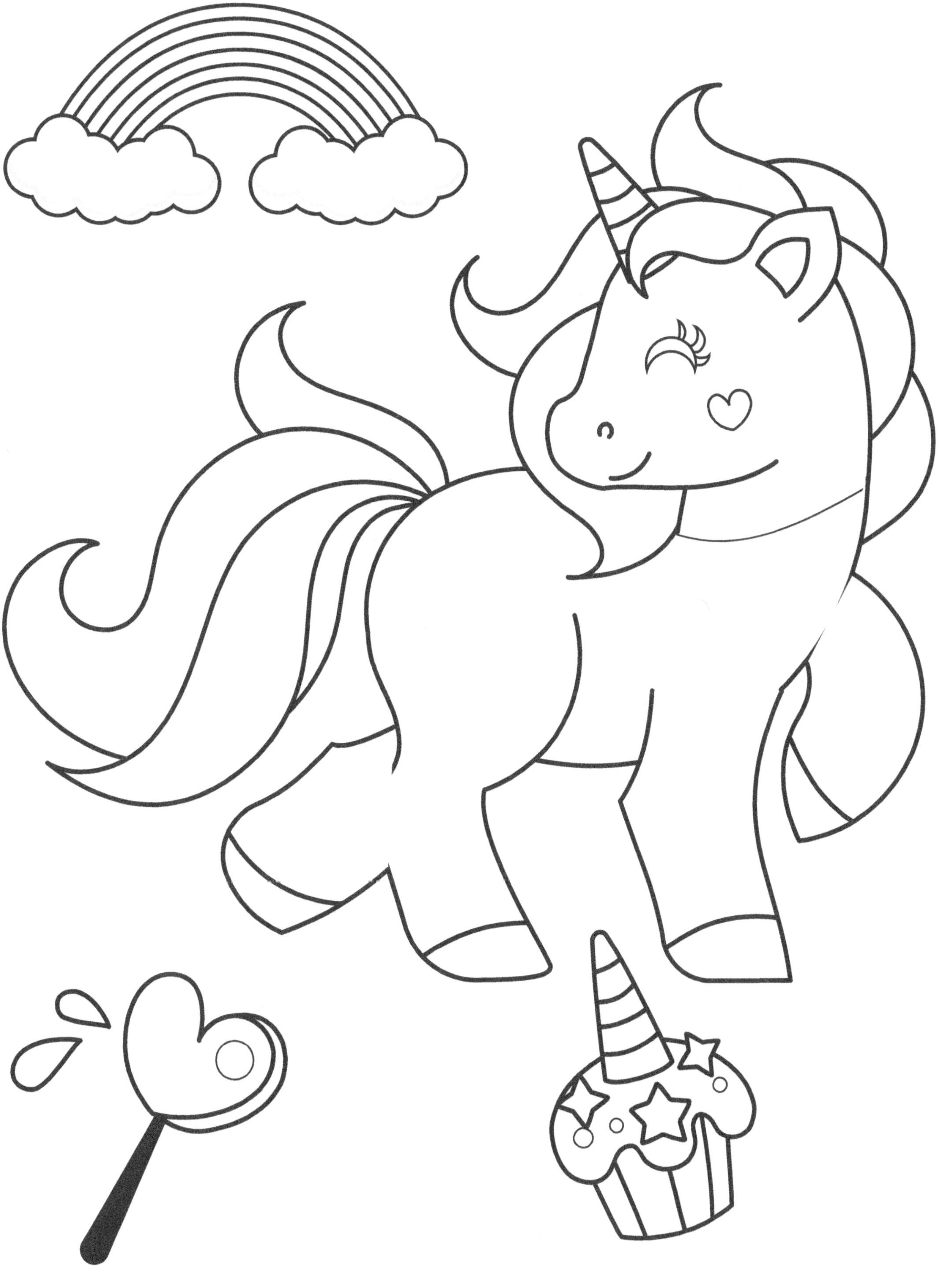

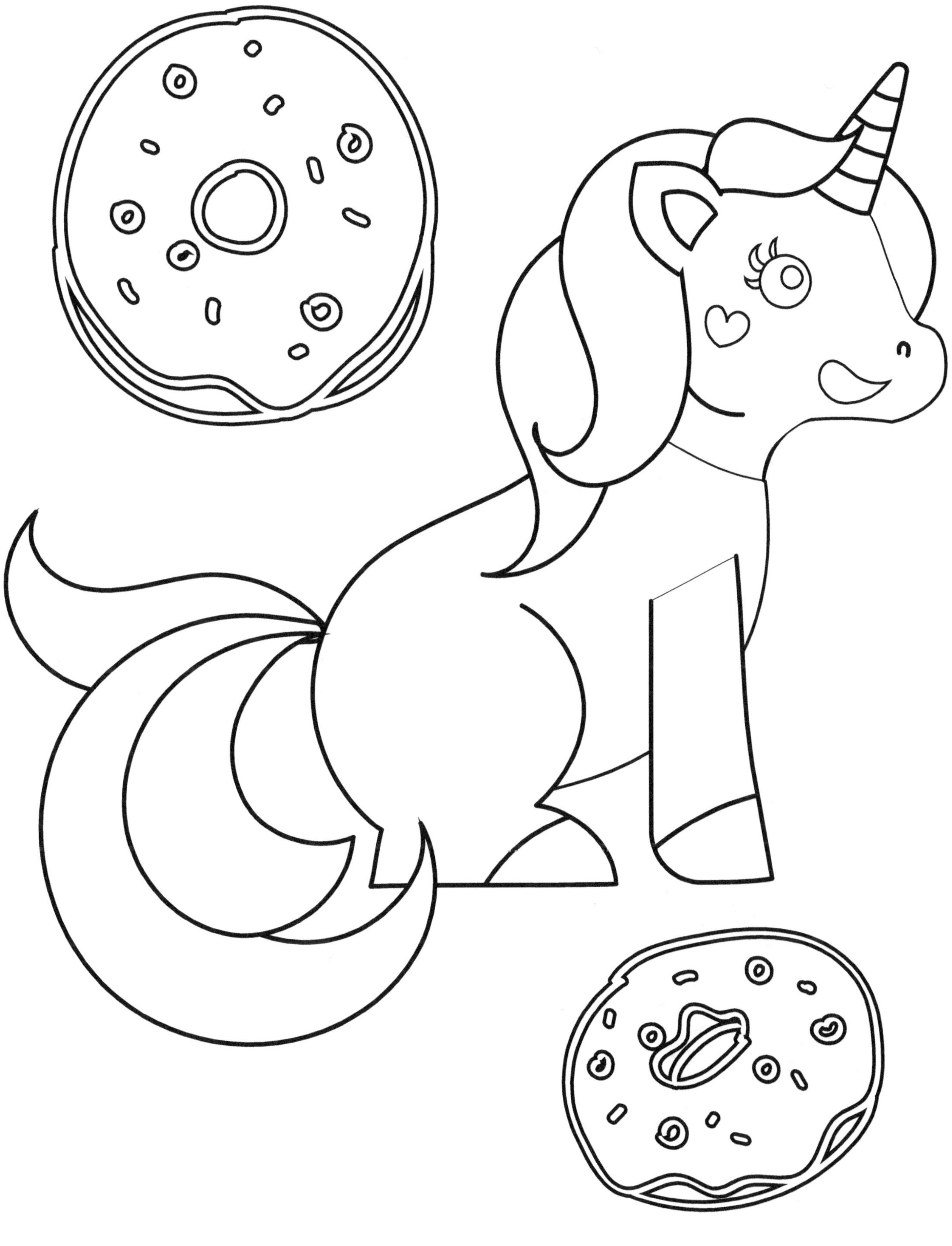

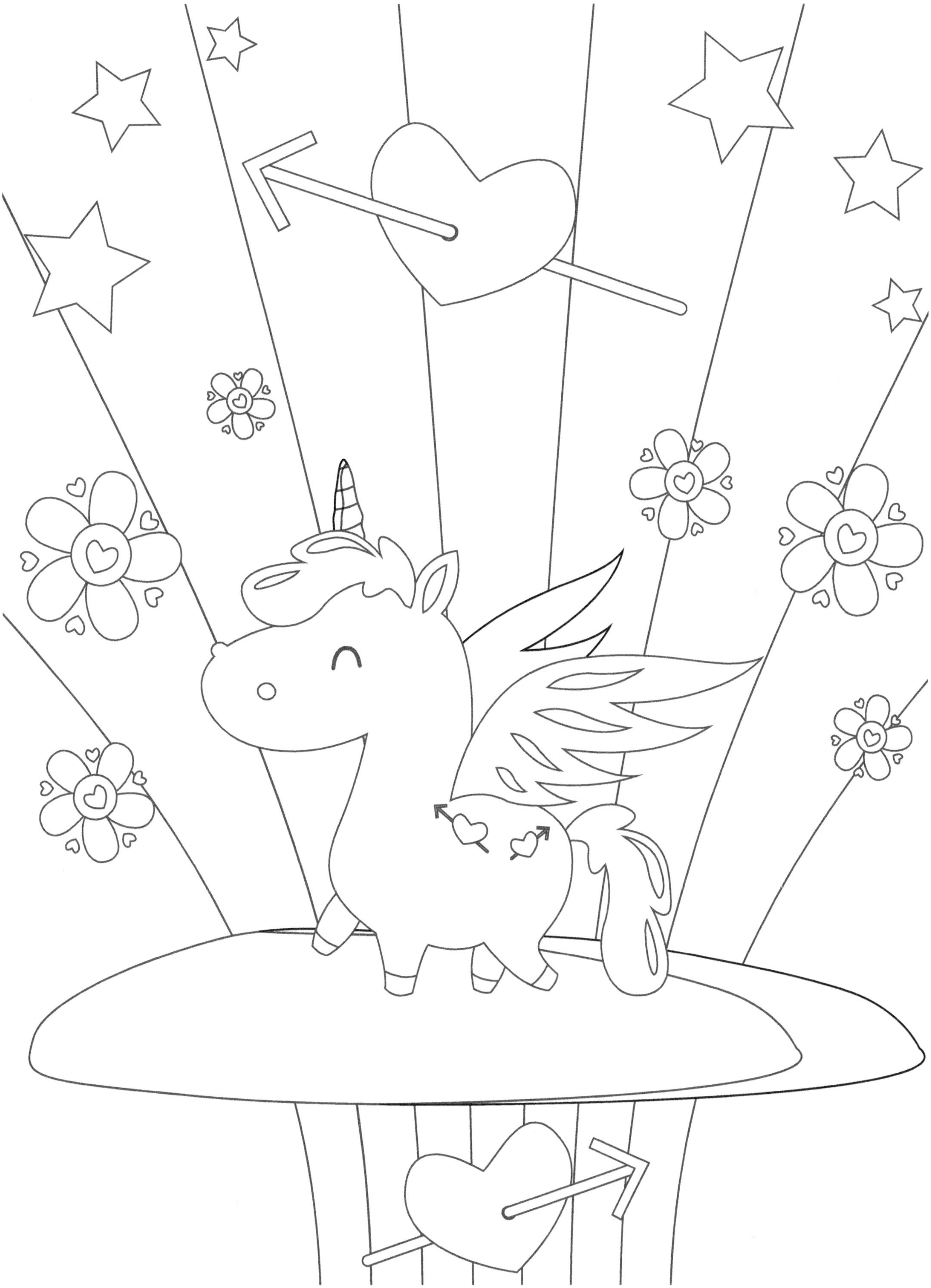

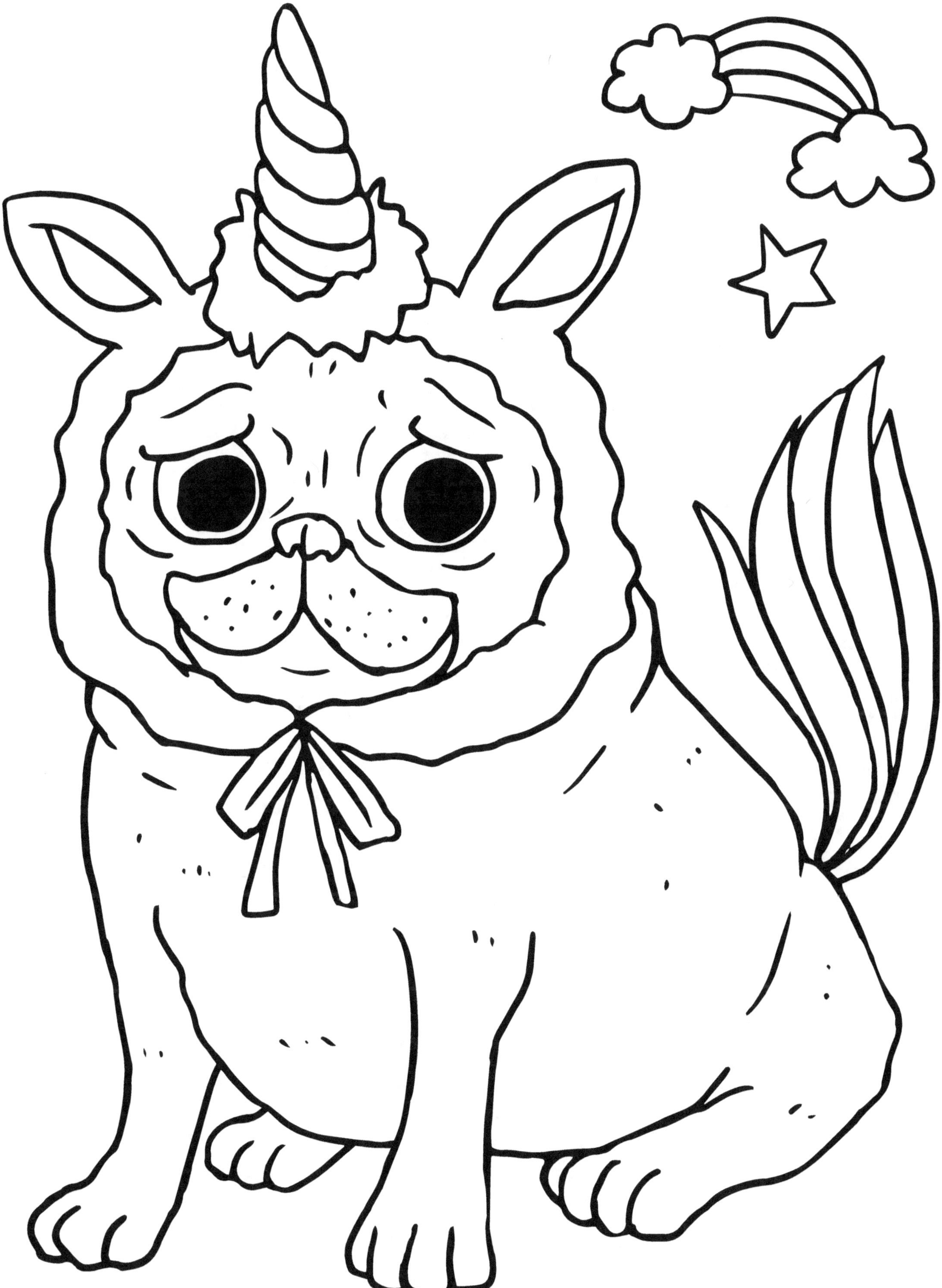

BORN TO BE A

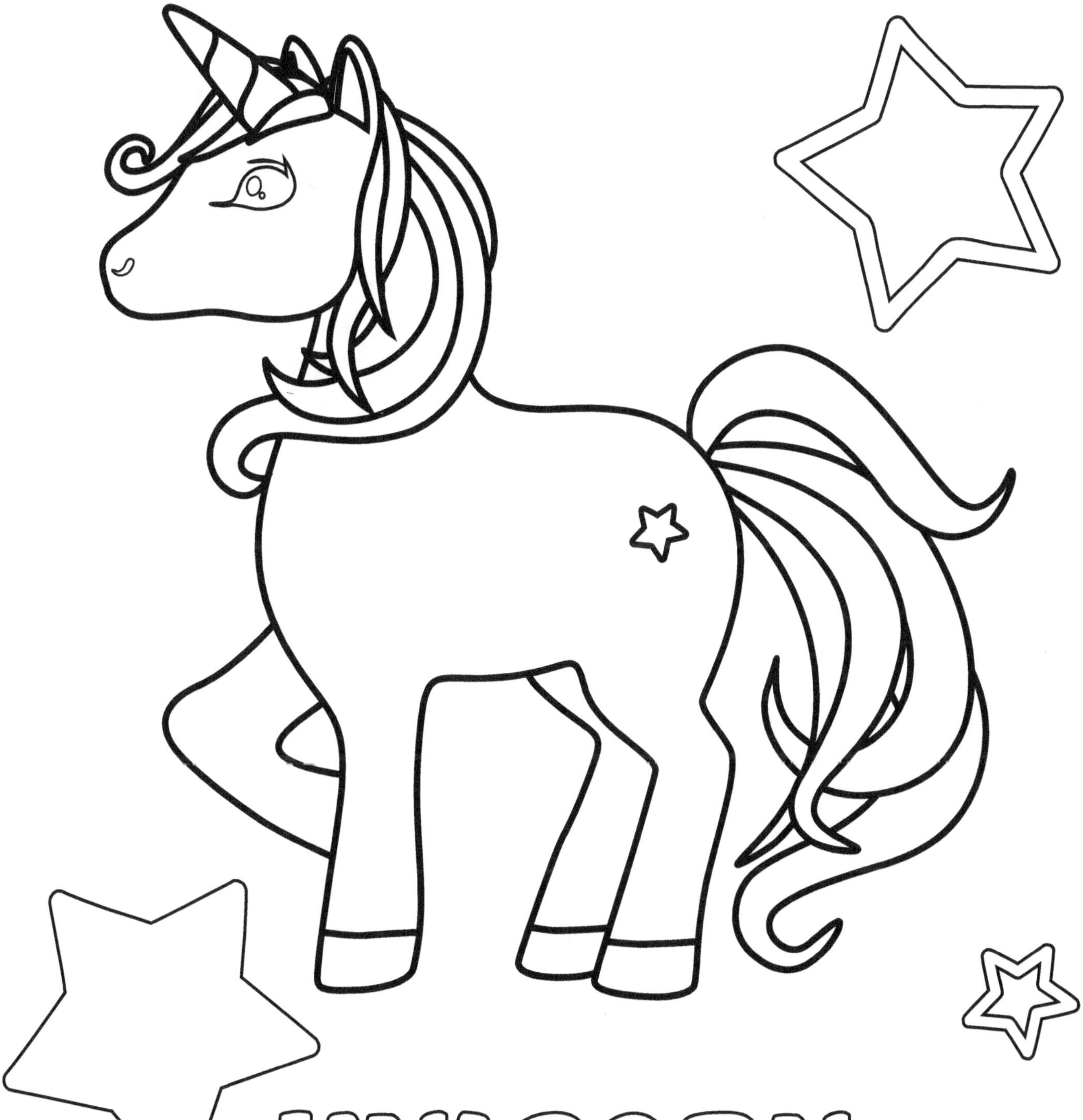

UNICORN

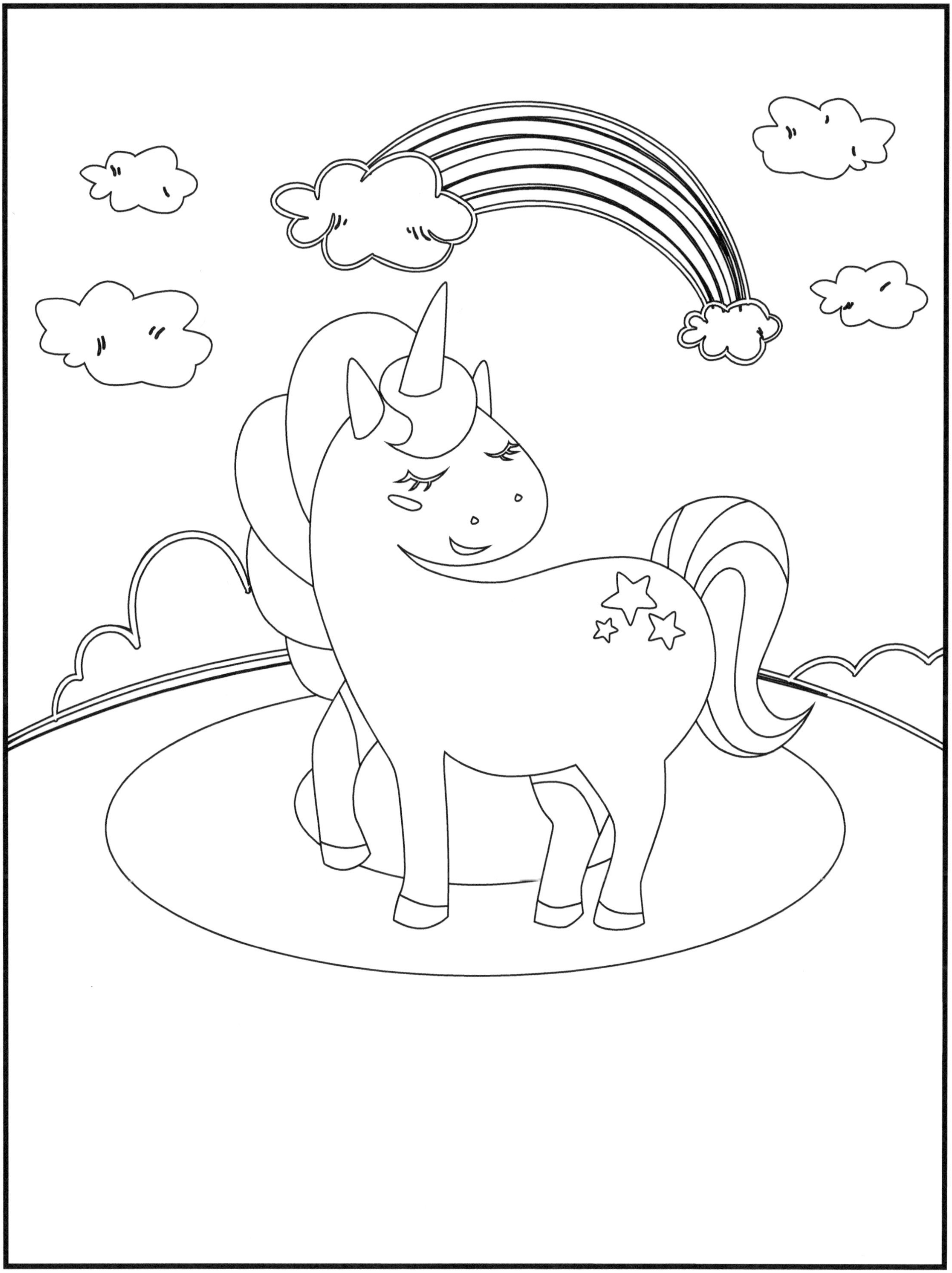

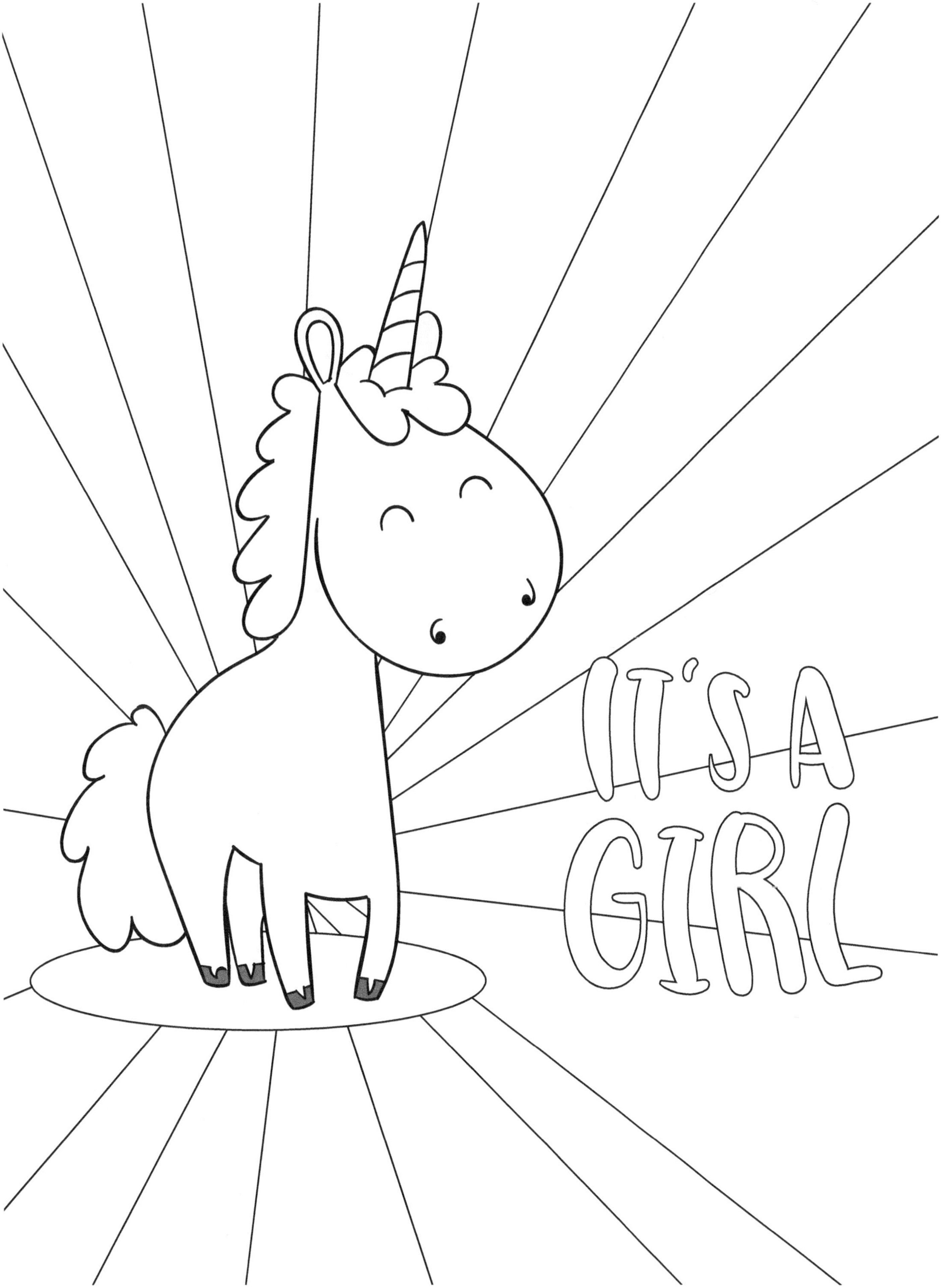
IT'S A
GIRL

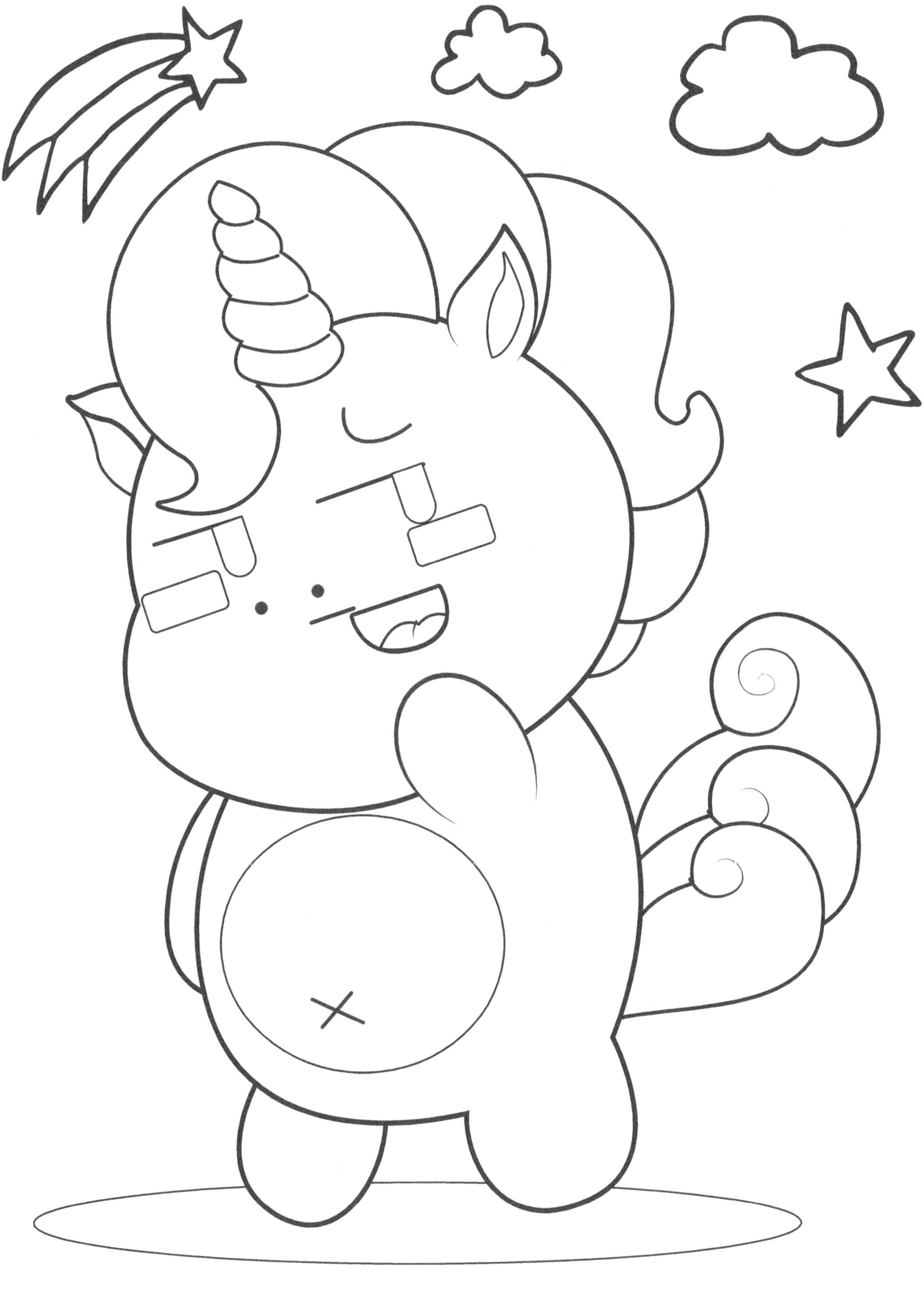

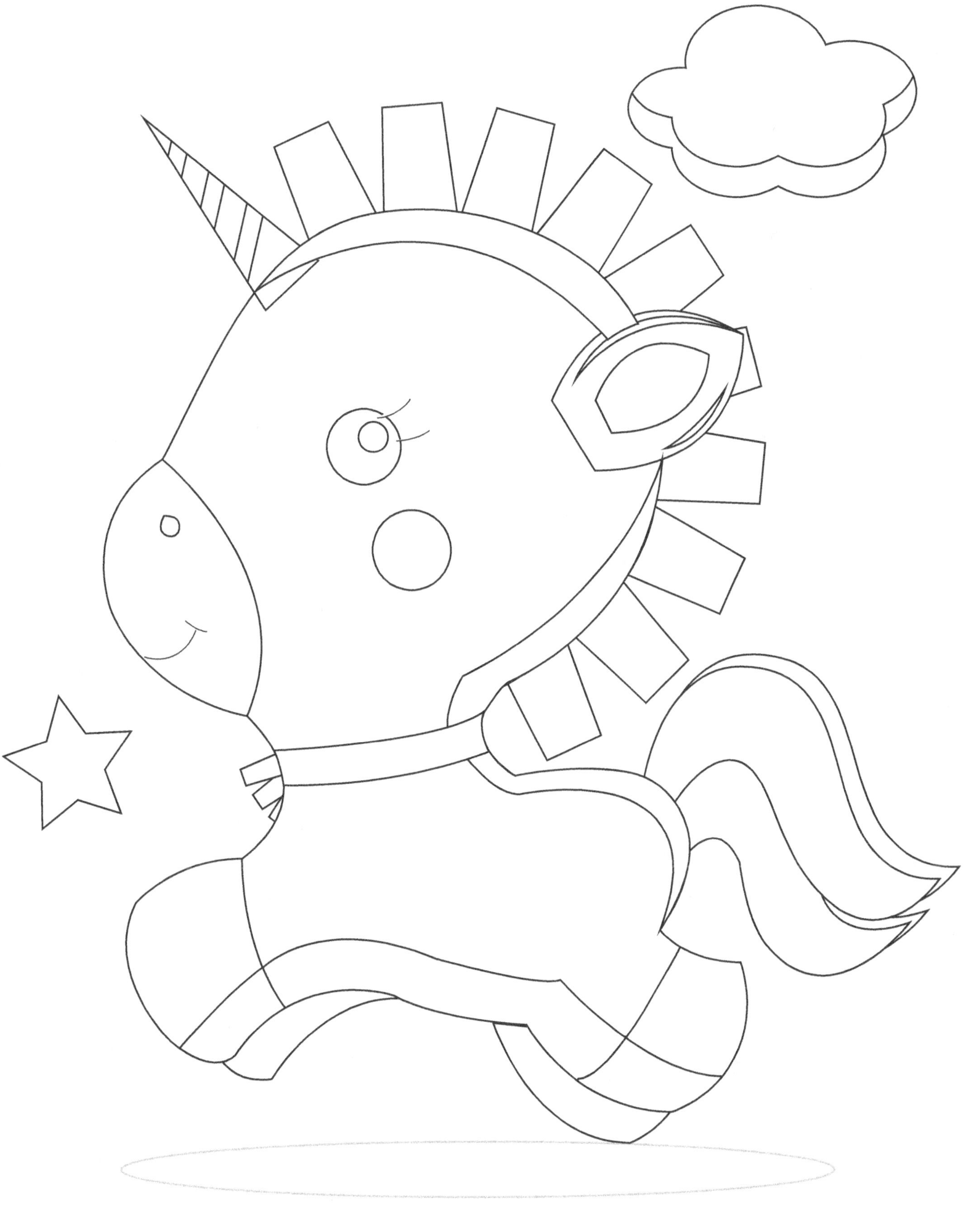

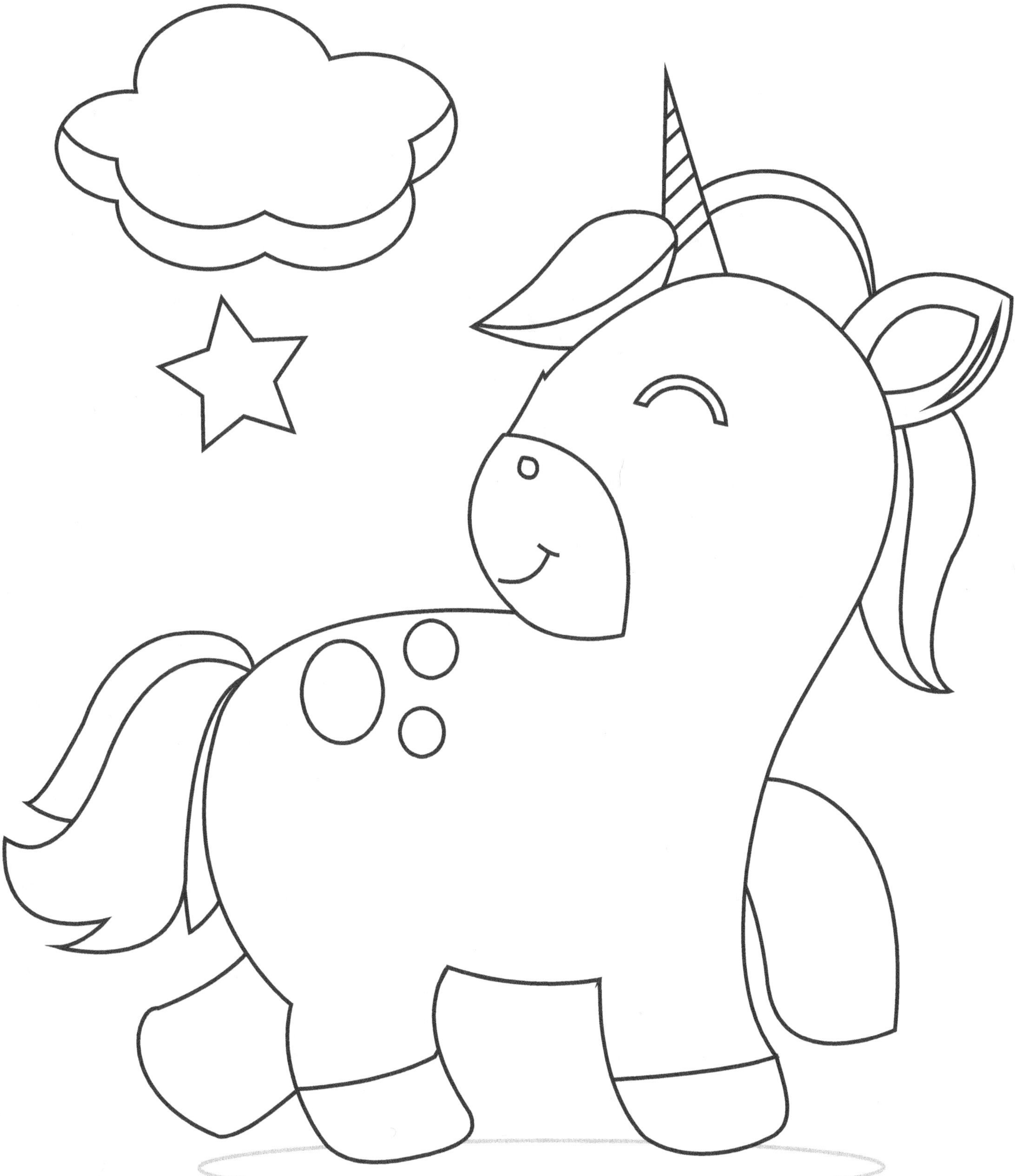

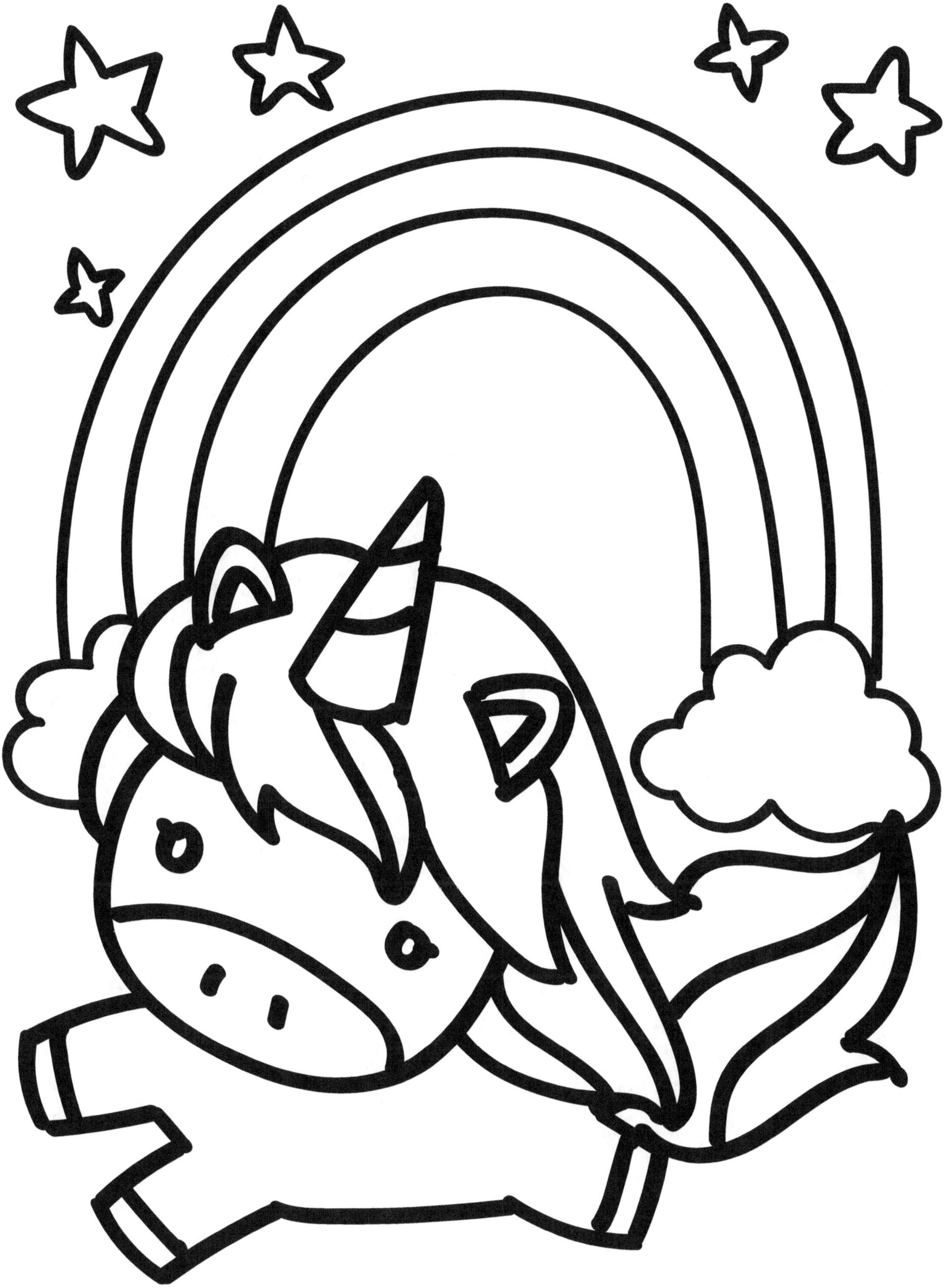

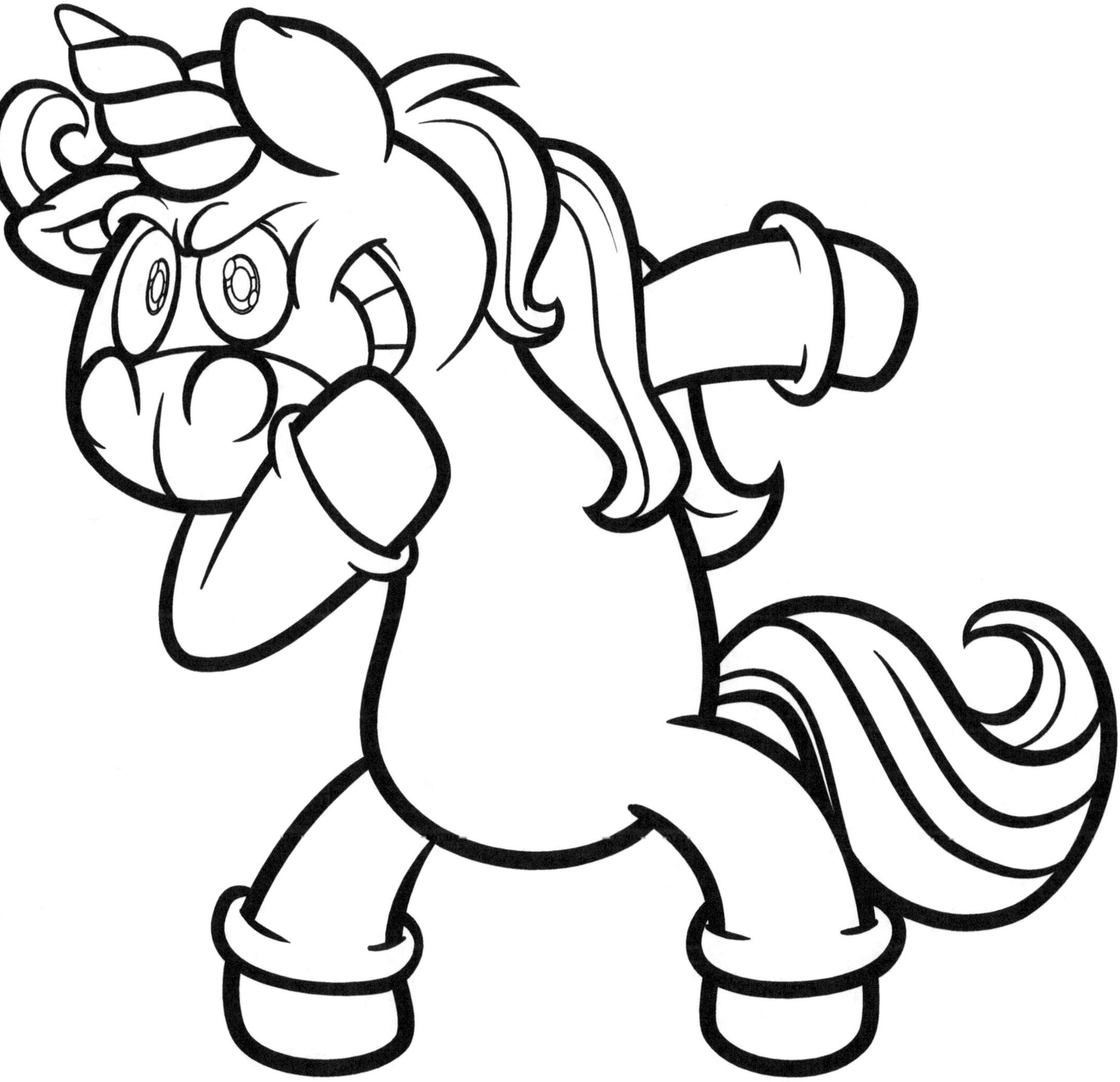

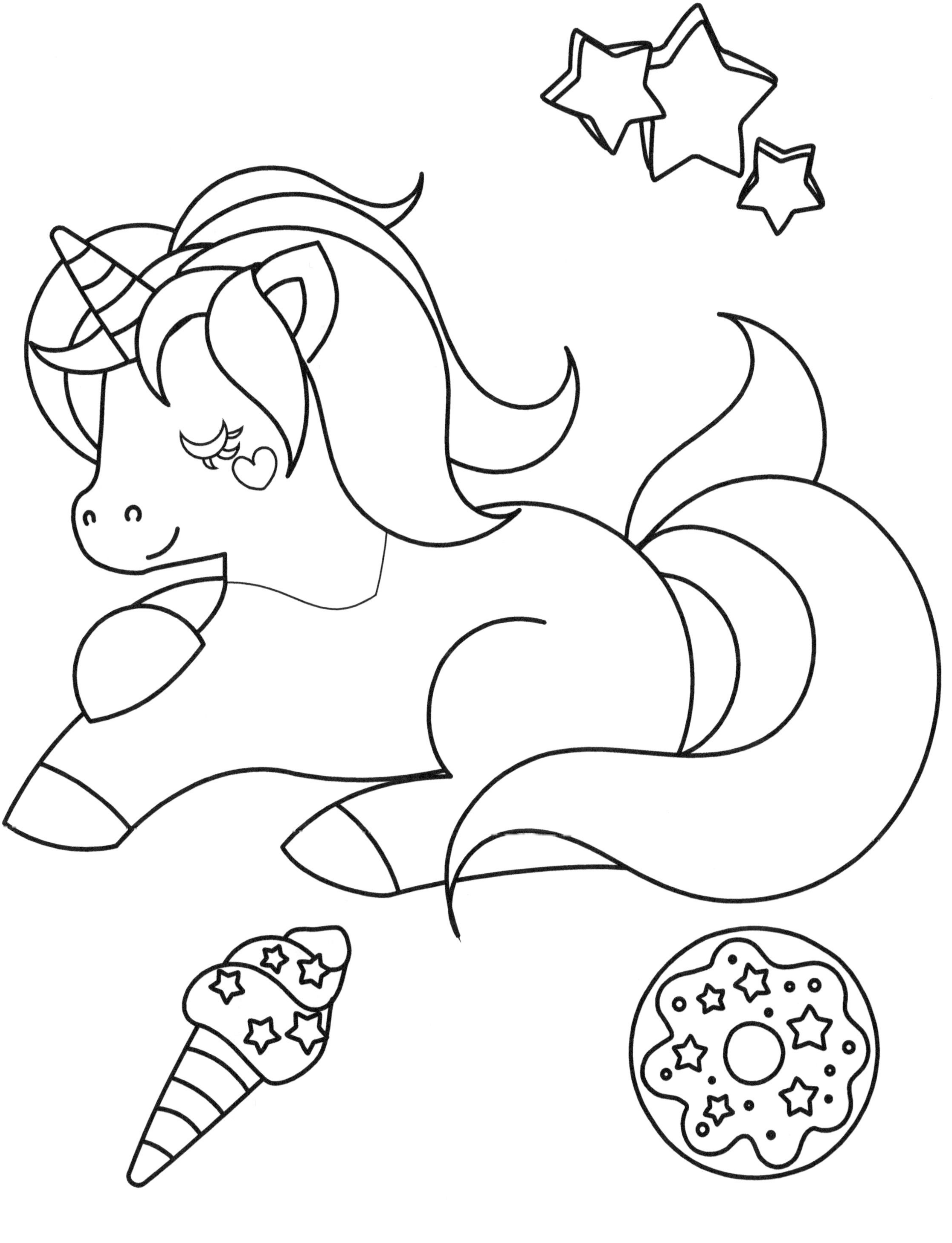

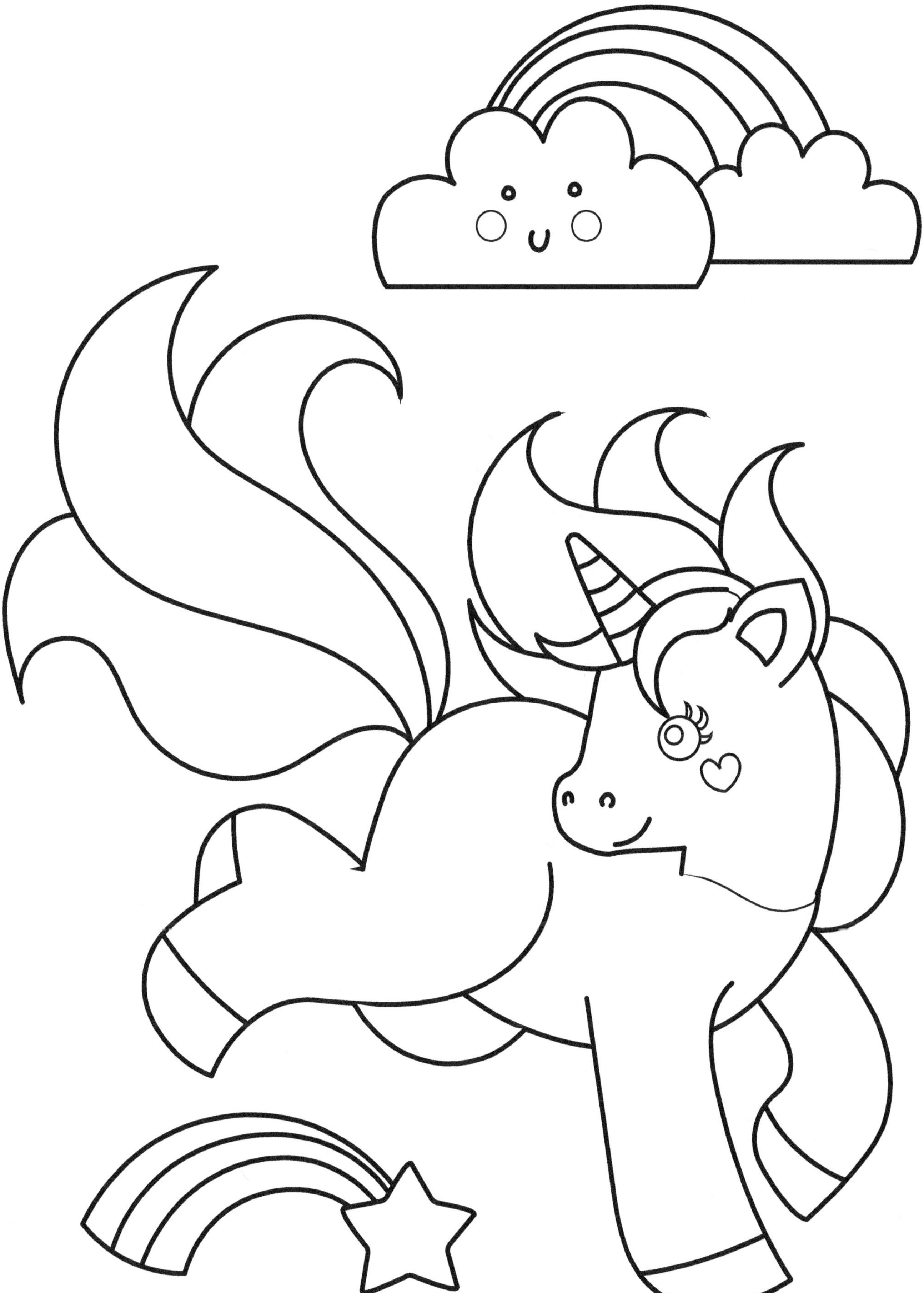

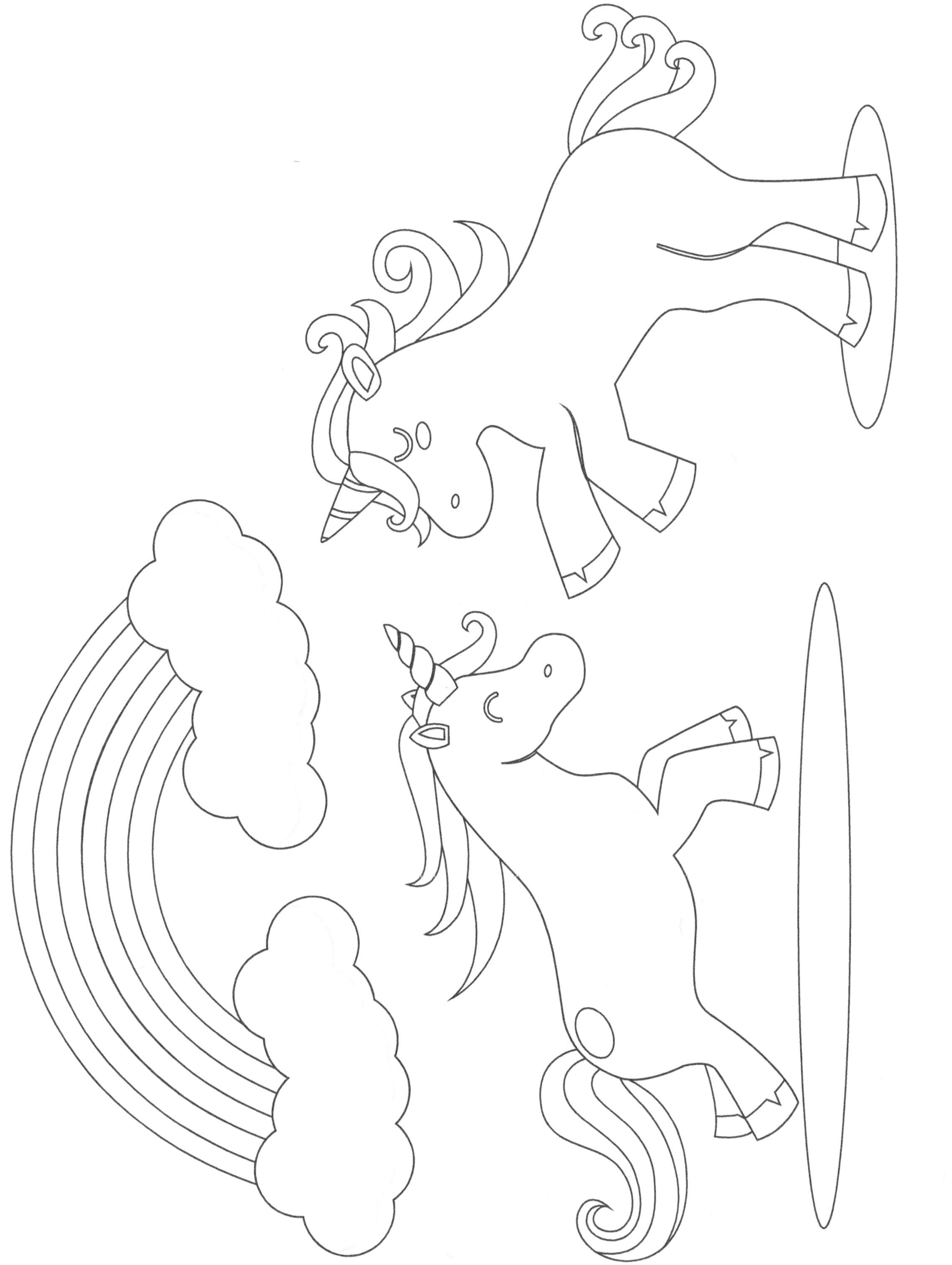

www.ingramcontent.com/pod-product-compliance
Lightning Source LLC
Chambersburg PA
CBHW080959220526
45467CB00008B/2623